My Three Sons

My Three Sons

LESTER SUMRALL

THOMAS NELSON PUBLISHERS
Nashville • Camden • New York

Published in Nashville, Tennessee, by Thomas Nelson, Inc. and distributed in Canada by Lawson Falle, Ltd., Cambridge, Ontario.

Printed in the United States of America.

ISBN 0-8407-5894-4

*This book is lovingly dedicated
to my wife Louise:
An excellent wife
A great mother
An affectionate grandmother*

Contents

Preface

Although this book is concerned primarily with the relationship between me and my sons, I do not mean to slight the mother's role in the home. I know that my wife, Louise, could write another volume about the vicissitudes of Christian motherhood.

Our sons would not be the men they are today were it not for a wonderful mother—a woman of faith, patience, and wisdom. In writing my story of a father's responsibility toward his children, I also want to emphasize that parenthood is a partnership. As you will see, beginning in the early chapters of this book, none of this could have been accomplished without Louise.

My sons and I salute her in the words of the wisest man:

> Her children rise up
>   and call her blessed;
> Her husband also, and he praises her:
> "Many daughters have done well
> But you excel them all."
> Prov. 31:28–29

Lester Sumrall
South Bend, Indiana

Introduction

It is a very difficult task to speak for at least five persons. It is more difficult when they are your family. Each one has a different view of the same event. Some of the important events in our family history are not included because they are not essential to the purpose of the book.

The grand purpose of this book is simple.

It was God who first created the family. In the Bible He outlined special laws relating only to this institution. He stressed that family unity is essential. To illustrate, Noah and his family united as one person in order to save the antediluvian civilization. God also made His tremendous promises to Abraham and his family as a result of his faithfulness.

In contrast, Lot and his divided family ultimately caused the destruction of Sodom and Gomorrah.

All of this shows that the family is the most important institution on earth.

Christ said "If a house is divided against itself, that kingdom cannot stand" (Mark 3:25). This means a united family will not fall.

In this book, we have recorded how God gave Louise and me three sons. These sons are the subject of this book. What I have said of my sons will please many families. Others it will not. All of us want all of you to know that in these unusual times it is still possible for the total family to live and work in the Spirit of Christ Jesus our Lord.

My Three Sons

1

Preparing for Fatherhood

A number of years ago in Howe, England, a friend of mine caught my arm and directed my attention toward a certain woman.

"That woman is involved in practices of the occult," he told me. "She practices spiritualism—trying to communicate with the dead."

I nodded. I had come across many like her.

"You'll never guess what kind of home she came from," he added.

"No, I suppose not," I said. "I can imagine all sorts of terrible things, but I would probably be wrong."

"She came from an outstanding Christian home," my friend said. "In fact, her father was the famous preacher, Charles H. Spurgeon."

I was shocked.

"I find that hard to believe," I said. "He was one of the greatest preachers who ever lived. How could this have happened to his own daughter? Wasn't she given a proper upbringing?"

"Oh, yes, but it didn't 'take'. You know how it is with so many children of famous preachers—and of ordinary preachers as well. They rebel against the strict upbringing of their parents and end up not Christians at all.

"After Spurgeon died, his daughter went to the spiritualists to try to contact her dead father. She has been involved in the occult ever since."

I was appalled. Here, among millions of deceived people, was the offspring of London's famous preacher, known world-wide for his evangelizing and laboring for God's kingdom. Yet his own daughter was not included in his heavenly harvest!

By that time I had already preached my way around the world. I had become infused with a zeal for souls as the result of two visions from God. The first vision had preceded my healing from tuberculosis and had resulted in my salvation and commitment to preach. The second came with my call to be a missionary: a vision of lost humanity marching relentlessly onward toward a lost eternity.

Although I was still single at the time, I had a very clear awareness of the importance of the Christian family. I did not want it to end like Charles Spurgeon's.

"Lord, if You ever give me a family," I prayed, "I am going to rear my children for You! I am going to do everything within my power to ensure that they will come into Your kingdom."

I decided then to prepare myself for becoming a husband and father. I committed myself to studying the Scriptures and the lives of well-known Christians to see what I could learn from them. Also, I envisioned the kind of family I wanted, so that I could pray, asking God to bring it about.

I was determined even then to prove that a busy evangelist and missionary could still take time to shepherd his own children into the kingdom of God.

That decision was made many years ago. It turned out to be one of the most important decisions of my life. Today I can testify that busy pastors can indeed bring up their children to be faithful to Christ. God gave me three wonderful sons who are not only fine Christians but also faithful coworkers in Christian evangelism.

In this book, I wish to tell the story of how it all came about.

Before I go on with the story, however, I want to state emphatically that this book is not an attempt on my part to set up the Sumrall family as an example for everyone to follow. Some will disagree with my philosophy in rearing children. The Sumrall family is not a perfect family, nor have my sons been angels all the time, as later chapters will show. I do not want to be judgmental and claim that I did everything right in bringing up my sons while others have taken the wrong approach. Each family is different, and its goals and interpretations of parenthood will vary.

What I do want to convey, though, is an honest, from-the-heart story of how one busy missionary family managed to devote enough time and attention to three energetic sons and have them turn out the way we believe God intended.

Others have had similar success. One of the best examples I know is General William Booth, founder of the Salvation Army. Booth's son William and daughter Evangeline both became generals in the Salvation Army. In addition, Evangeline went on to become one of the greatest preachers France has ever known.

Another example of a successful family is the Wesley family in England. John and Charles Wesley were sons of a priest in the Church of England. Both of them far exceeded any spiritual goals their parents may have set for them.

There have been many other fine examples through the years of sons and daughters who have followed their parents into missionary and evangelistic work. Yet the sad statistic that has been reported to me is that two-thirds of all pastors and evangelists lose their own children—some to outright unbelief and others to ineffective witnessing for Jesus Christ.

Among the latter, for instance, is a minister who had been rearing his son to succeed him in a major ministry. He was also planning for his daughter to become the church secretary. However, as the children grew, they resisted being pressed into the mold their father had shaped for them. Even the minister's wife balked, arguing that the children should be able to make up their own minds about what they wanted to do.

In the end, neither child stayed with the ministry. The son wanted to go into business for himself, so the father bought him a service station. The daughter went to work in a bank. Both drifted from the faith and into unhappy marriages which later ended in divorce.

I cannot condemn the minister for the way he reared his children, any more than I can judge Charles Spurgeon for what he did or did not do. I do not have all the facts. But I am grieved by the overwhelming loss of children from influential Christian homes—children who become enemies of the church, or who apathetically drift into drugs and alcohol, or who choose the fleeting pleasures of materialism and want nothing to do with the church.

I pray that some of the ideas put forth in this book will save the newer generations.

Back in the 1930s I had very little time to think about a family. I had joined up with British Bible scholar Howard Carter, and the two of us traveled literally around the world, ministering in places such as New Zealand, Australia, Indonesia, Singapore, Korea, Japan, China, and Europe. We had also traveled by train across Siberia and

Russia. On my own, I later ministered in Alaska and throughout Latin America.

I had spent over thirteen years, ministering around the world, without a family. Yet I believed that "It is not good that the man should be alone" (Gen. 2:18). I knew that civilization had been founded—and is based—not on individuals but on families. God's promises to Abraham were for a family—that he should become "a great nation."

I had first become aware of the importance of the Christian family several years earlier, when I was only nineteen. I had been preaching in various states, and in Oklahoma a couple came to me for counseling. They had just been saved. They were brand new Christians, but they were extremely upset.

"This is the second marriage for both of us," the wife said. "Each of us had been divorced when we met, and we have children from our former marriages."

The husband added, "And we also have a child together."

The wife continued, "Some Christians have told us that because divorce is wrong, we have to break up this marriage and go back to live with our former spouses."

She was on the verge of tears. As I said, I was only nineteen and completely inexperienced in marital counseling. The couple could have made a great mistake in coming to me, for the wrong advice might have ruined their future lives.

Silently I prayed, asking God for wisdom before I answered.

"No," I said. "God doesn't want you to go back. You start at the point of your salvation and go forward. You can't return to your former lives."

They were so happy they could have crushed me with

love. And I was happy that God had given me wisdom. Now this family could stay together and live godly lives from that point on.

I cannot remember how old I was when I began to ask God seriously about helping me to find the right wife, but I do know that as I approached the age of thirty, I began to envision just what kind of family I wanted. Of course, it would have to be a biblical family, and my wife would have to be a believer. Still, what did God require of me? I had to be prepared, too.

I do not know how many men consciously prepare themselves for fatherhood before they are married, but I doubt it is a very large percentage. No one had ever counseled me about preparing for fatherhood. It seemed that the man was just expected to know what to do when the time came. However, in reading the Bible, I saw that God had placed great importance on families, and upon the man as the head of the family. I knew I faced a great responsibility.

Early in my preparation I became aware of the importance of the father image. The Bible says that God created man in His own image. God is our Father, and we often relate to God in ways we have learned through relating to our earthly fathers. The kind of image a child has of his father can become a doorway or a barrier to relating to God. If a child loses faith in his father, he practically loses faith in the human race—and perhaps in God as well.

I remember the way I viewed my own father when I was a boy. He was a six-foot, two-inch machinist who was physically very strong. I recall hanging onto his arm while he raised me up and held me straight out in front of him. Once I even saw him do that with a grown man. He had the man sit in a chair; then my father picked up the chair with two hands, grasping it by the legs, and held it at arm's length in front of him—with the man still sitting in it.

I loved my father. I still remember the day he took me to the barber shop for my first haircut. The barber put me on a small stool on the chair, wrapped a cloth around my neck, and asked, "Lester, how do you want your hair cut?"

I looked up at him and said, in a proud, self-assured voice, "Just like Papa's."

The men in the barber shop laughed. I was embarrassed, but what else could I say? I wanted to be just like my daddy.

As I was praying to have a family, I knew I wanted sons who would look up to me just like that, who would emulate me. That meant I would have to be a leader.

Today Western society has robbed some men of leadership in the home. Often it is a result of the wife's going out to work. She sometimes makes more money than her husband, and rivalry over decision making results. The husband's role is weakened.

According to the Bible, though, the man is to act not only as decision maker in matters pertaining to discipline, finances, and other earthly concerns but also as spiritual leader in the home. Yet many men—even those in Christian families—are embarrassed to pray with their wives and children. They see that as a form of weakness, when instead it is the family's greatest source of strength.

The Bible told me that my leadership in the church would be determined by my leadership in the home. Paul wrote to Timothy:

A bishop then must be blameless, the husband of one wife, temperate, sober-minded, of good behavior, hospitable, able to teach; . . . One who rules his own house well, having his children in submission with all reverence (for if a man does not know how to rule his own house, how will he take care of the church of God?) (1 Tim. 3:2, 4–5).

To me, those verses mean more than just discipline and moral behavior. A pastor should lead his own household just as he leads the church, for there is a great spiritual parallel between the family and the church.

If I wanted to be a good husband and father, I would have to take the leadership role spiritually in the family God would give me. It meant more than just praying and being a spiritual example to my family. I would have to look after its total spiritual well-being.

I knew the devil was trying harder than ever to destroy the family. He had begun by weakening the man as head of the house. He knew that as the man becomes weaker, the home itself begins to weaken. In some modern homes, the men lose their sense of responsibility. They often fall into moral weakness and perhaps even become dependent on alcohol. Adultery may follow. The results are broken homes and divorce.

One of the laws of the universe is that if a man does not live according to the laws of God he forfeits his headship in the home and loses his leadership.

The character of leadership is not something that can be put on or taken off to suit the occasion. Character is built. It becomes an integral part of one's life, making one's decisions, actions, and responses consistent.

Almost all children view their fathers with admiration if there is strength and consistency of inner character. They are looking for dependable qualities. I saw those qualities in the men I admired, in biographies I read, and in the Bible. I knew I would have to maintain them.

The first dependable quality is honesty. For a child to trust his father, he needs to know that his father tells the truth. This is a reflection of Psalm 25:5, which begins, "Lead me in Your truth, and teach me."

The second quality is integrity. A father cannot say one thing and do another. If a man makes a big show of loving his wife and family, yet is having a secret affair with another woman, he has lost his integrity. Sooner or later he will be found out, and the effect on the child will be devastating. A man cannot bring up his children properly without integrity. Psalm 5:8 states, "Lead me, O LORD, in Your righteousness." Righteousness includes our integrity.

Finally, a leader needs to have ability. That is a quality that is particularly needed in fathers. Ability to teach. Ability to show the way. Ability to fix things or make things right. A child likes nothing better than to know he can go to his father with his problems or his broken toys, because Dad has the ability to fix it or to make it better. Isaiah 48:17 says, "I am the LORD your God who teaches you to profit, who leads you by the way that you should go." As fathers, we are to reflect godly qualities of leadership by being able to teach and to show the way. If we do not, the result can be disaster.

One of the saddest cases in Scripture of a father's not carrying out his leadership responsibilities toward his children is that of the priest Eli in First Samuel. Eli had reared his sons as priests to succeed him at Shiloh, but the sons certainly did not acquire the qualities of leadership from their father that God or the people expected of them. They sent servants to fish out the best portions of the sacrifices for their own tables (see 1 Sam. 2:12–17), and they even had intercourse with women who assembled at the gates of the tabernacle (see v. 22). Although Eli reprimanded his sons, they did not listen to him, and

Eli did not punish them or remove them from office. Finally the Lord spoke to the boy Samuel and gave him a message for Eli: God himself would judge Eli and his family for failing to stop the sin (see 1 Sam. 3:14). Even then Eli did not act. He simply replied, "It is the LORD: let him do what seems good to him" (v.18). As a result, Eli and his two sons all died on the same day (see 1 Sam. 4).

To me this illustrates perfectly the awesome responsibility of fatherhood. Eli was held accountable for the behavior of his sons, who were sinning against the Lord. Although he reprimanded them, he did nothing to bring about a change. One can surmise that Eli had not taken the time to rear his sons properly, and he had not earned enough of their respect so that they would obey him.

I realized that God would hold me accountable for the upbringing of my children. I would be responsible to be both an example and a leader for them. I would also be responsible for their physical, mental, and spiritual upbringing, so that they would grow up healthy in body, mind, and spirit.

Of course, even Scripture does not promise that is is possible for a father to be 100 percent successful in rearing his children in the fear and service of the Lord. Adam's firstborn son became a murderer. Jacob's sons sold their brother Joseph into Egyptian captivity. David's firstborn son, Amnon, raped his half-sister and was in turn murdered by her brother, Absalom.

On the other hand, many fathers in the Bible were rewarded for their attention to their children. Abraham's faithfulness, both to God and to his family, allowed God's promise to be carried out. He became the father of a great nation. He was even careful to arrange for his son Isaac to marry a girl from within the covenant family (see Gen. 24).

David, of course, produced Solomon. There was also the faithful priest Zechariah who became the father of John the Baptist.

Godly fathers can indeed produce godly offspring, but it requires attention and concentration in loving them and in training them properly. Proverbs 22:6 says, "Train up a child in the way he should go, and when he is old, he will not depart from it." I read this verse to mean that even though the child may rebel for a while, he eventually will come back and be faithful to his early training. The story of the prodigal son (see Luke 15:11–32) is a perfect example from the parables of Jesus.

As much as I saw the importance of rearing a godly family, however, during those early years of my life, I moved around too often to look for the right girl to marry. I decided that if I was to have a wife and family God would have to provide them. I prayed earnestly that God would bring me the right woman, and that when we met I would know she was the right one.

There were some requirements to be met, of course. First of all, she would have to be a strong Christian who would approve and encourage me in my ministry of missionary evangelism. Because of this world ministry, it would have been unthinkable to consider a woman who was not wholeheartedly committed to Jesus Christ.

She would have to have a vision for evangelism and missionary work. She would have to be so enthusiastic in her faith that she not only would encourage me and pray for my ministry but also labor beside me to win souls for Jesus Christ. In addition to that, she would become the mother of my children—children I wanted to grow up strong in the faith—and I would need her to help me provide the proper spiritual and moral leadership in the home.

I first met Louise Layman in late 1942 at a wedding in Buenos Aires, Argentina, but our paths had crossed a number of times in the preceding couple of years. She, too, was a missionary who had traveled widely in North and South America, and once we had missed each other by only a few hours in Prince Rupert, British Columbia. I had heard her praised by some mutual missionary acquaintances, and she had heard me minister on HCJB, the Christian shortwave station in Quito, Ecuador. But until then we had never met.

I was very interested in the striking young woman I saw playing the organ at the wedding in Buenos Aires. I asked a missionary friend to introduce us. As she smiled in my direction even before the introduction was made, I felt God was already speaking to my heart. While we chatted, I had the strangest desire to remain with her always.

We met a second time shortly afterward at her mission station about seven hours by train outside of Buenos Aires. I was surprised upon my arrival there, for a speaking engagement during the Christmas season, to find a present with my name on it under the mission Christmas tree. It was a little wooden donkey from Louise Layman. I promptly named it "Luisa," which is the Spanish version of Louise.

During the next year we corresponded, and finally I asked her—by mail—to become my wife. In March 1944 I received her reply. She accepted! It was the greatest thrill of my life since the day I had decided to follow Jesus.

It still amazes me how God prepared Louise and me to be a beautifully matched couple, and then brought us together in a place so remote from our original homes. Although I had grown up in the South and Louise had grown up in Canada, we had been born only fourteen days apart. We had received Christ as our personal Savior as teenagers and had committed ourselves to Christian ministry. We had gone into missionary service in the same month of the same year, Louise to Argentina, and I to depart America for New Zealand and Australia.

Louise had the same vision for souls that I had. Together we spent the first two years of our marriage on a remarkable fifty-thousand-mile honeymoon, traveling throughout the West Indies and South America to preach the gospel. We were one—not only as husband and wife but also as missionaries with a burning desire to see souls saved for the kingdom of God. Although our personalities were completely different (I am very outgoing while she is more reserved), we thought alike and both had the same concerns about rearing a family.

Louise and I have been married for forty years. In our American society we are rareties. How many people, even in the church of Jesus Christ, remain married to each for forty years? I thank God for His selection of a wife for me!

2

Becoming a Father

Just before breakfast the telephone rang in my hotel room in St. Louis. I wondered if it could be Louise calling me. Although it was the morning of New Year's Eve, December 31, 1946, Louise was across the state at our home in Springfield, Missouri, expecting our first child in just ten days. I did not like being separated from her, because for more than two years since our wedding we had rarely been apart. Now I was speaking at a series of meetings in Bethel Temple, and Louise was too far along in her pregnancy to think of traveling long distances. We had traveled all through the West Indies and South America as missionary evangelists, but now we had purchased a house in Springfield, while I ministered as an itinerant evangelist and Louise awaited the birth of our first child.

I picked up the telephone and heard my sister saying, "Lester, this is Leona. Mother has just taken Louise to the hospital. The baby's coming!"

It was too soon! I had planned my speaking schedule so that I could be home at the time the baby was due, but now the baby was coming ten days early. My heart began to pound with excitement.

"I'll be right there," I said, and hung up the phone.

I had my car with me, but Springfield was more than

two hundred miles away. There was little likelihood that I would get there in time for the baby to be born if I spent four hours on the highway. I grabbed my overcoat, ran from the hotel, and jumped into the first taxi waiting outside.

"Take me to the airport," I told the driver. "And hurry. I have to catch a plane. My wife's having a baby!"

At the terminal I rushed up to the ticket counter. The schedule said the next plane for Springfield would be leaving in fifteen minutes.

"A ticket to Springfield," I said breathlessly. "I have to make that plane!"

The ticket agent looked at me very seriously. "I'm sorry, sir," he said, "but that flight is full."

"Well, then, put someone off the plane!" I said excitedly. "I have to get to Springfield. My wife's having a baby right now, and I have to be there with her and my son!"

The baby had not even been born yet, but already I was certain it was a boy.

The ticket agent was unimpressed, however.

"Sir, I can sell you a ticket," he said, "but all I can do is put you on standby. All the seats are taken. If one of the passengers doesn't show up, then I'll put you on the plane."

I bought the ticket and began to pray. I knew I had to be there with my wife and new baby. Surely God would provide the way!

At the last minute the agent called me over.

"We've had a no-show, Mr. Sumrall," he said. "You can get on the plane. It's right through that gate."

As the pilot revved up the prop-driven engines of the DC-3 and began to move away from the terminal, I buckled my seatbelt and settled back, thanking God for His provision. Then, while the plane was taxiing toward the runway, I thought back over the preceding year and remembered how hard Louise and I had been praying for this, our first child. After two years of marriage, we were both ready to have a family. We began praying and planning for children. Louise and I were healthy young adults; now was our time to have children. We wanted them.

At that time I did not ask for a son. In fact, Louise wanted a daughter very badly. I would have been just as happy with a daughter, and I felt it was not up to me to demand of the Lord that our first child be a boy.

When the doctor confirmed that Louise was pregnant, we began to pray even more intensely. Both of us were well aware of the spiritual forces at work in the world, and we knew children needed to be protected from the wrong ones. Each day I laid my hand on my wife's abdomen, she put her hand on top of mine, and together we prayed over the child developing within her.

"Lord, let this child be healthy," I prayed. "We realize that this child is a gift from You, and we want to rear it for You. We want it to grow up and be Your child, to stand and praise You. Lord, please accept this child back from us as our gift to You. We don't want to bring it up for the world, for some secular purpose. If we were going to do that, we wouldn't have asked for a child at all. Lord, let this child be blessed and grow up to work for Jesus."

Again and again, day after day during Louise's pregnancy, we continued to pray like that.

Along with our prayers we also studied the Scriptures and were comforted by verses such as, "Before I formed you in the womb I knew you; Before you were born I sanctified you; And I ordained you a prophet to the nations" (Jer. 1:5).

We also began to plan for the child. We had bought an old two-story house in Springfield and had moved into the first floor, while renting out the second floor to some students at Central Bible Institute. Now, with the baby's coming, we began converting one of the downstairs rooms into a nursery and furnishing it with a crib and other baby things.

By now I was really looking forward to being a father. I looked with joy and anticipation to the day when the baby would come into the world. I felt that its birth would bring a new purpose and fulfillment to my own life. At last I would be able to have the kind of family I had envisioned: a family devoted to God, a family that would be a blessing to Him and to the church.

In less than an hour the airplane was back on the ground, and I hurried through the Springfield terminal to look for a taxicab. I wanted to get to the hospital as quickly as possible.

There was a cab at the curb, and I jumped in and gave the driver instructions, adding, "Hurry, please. My wife's having a baby."

The driver did hurry, and I had barely arrived at the hospital and given my name to the receptionist when the doctor came out and said, "Congratulations, Reverend Sumrall! You have a son!"

A nurse followed and handed me the little pink-faced bundle.

I was in ecstasy! I was certain the little fellow, with fringes of reddish hair, looked just like me.

"How's my wife?" I asked.

"Just fine," the doctor replied. "She hasn't come out from under the anesthetic yet, but she'll be waking soon. Come this way."

It was a thrill for me to be there as Louise began to stir,

and I kissed her as I said, "Honey, we have a son." Then the two of us thanked and praised God.

That afternoon I went home and prepared to do something I had never heard of any other parent's doing. I decided to write a letter to my new son. I was so overjoyed that I wanted to preserve that moment. I wanted to tell my son just how I felt about him when he was born and to make a commitment to him. I did not know how long he would live—or how long I would live, for that matter—or what kind of person he would turn out to be. But I wanted to tell him I loved him, and I wrote this letter out of the joy of my heart:

My Dearest Son,

You have no name yet, but you will have as soon as I discuss it with your precious mother.

My son, you are wanted to become a part of this home. In this home you will always be welcome. Here you will share whatever there is to be shared.

Here you can speak freely and feel uninhibited.

Here you can take time to grow and to think, and to feel and to mature.

It is in a Christian home where real men are made, and possibly we should say that it is in the unchristian home where society's problem people are made.

We trust you will always love your home more than any other place, and that you will always feel happy being here.

I trust you will always respect your home and feel that it is a castle for our family . . . that you will never violate it and that you will hold it as a sacred place.

May you always come here to rest.

May you always come here to rejoice.

May our home be the happiest place in all of your living on this earth.

With deepest love,

Your daddy whom you will soon come
to know,
Lester Sumrall

I did not mail the letter, of course. I put it in my files,
saving it for the day when my son would be old enough to
understand the significance of what I had written.

The next day Louise and I named him Frank Lester
Sumrall.

I wanted Frank to have all the advantages I never had. I
had gone into the ministry with sixty-five cents in my
pocket, but I had a keen business mind and knew the importance of trading and investments. As a youngster in
Laurel, Mississippi, I had bought hundred-pound sacks of
fresh peanuts, roasted the nuts in my mother's oven, then
put them into little individual bags and sold them to the
workers at the sawmill nearby.

I never capitalized on my business sense—not in the
ways of worldly money-making, that is. You see, at the
age of seventeen I was miraculously healed of tuberculosis
after having received a vision from God—a vision in
which I was given a choice of a casket or the Bible. I had
chosen the Bible and promised the Lord I would preach
for Him, and the next day I was healed.

Yet, over the years God had blessed my ministry financially as well as spiritually. I learned to use the Lord's
money wisely, and I knew the value of investing for a future return.

With that thought in mind, I decided to set something
aside for Frank's future. I went out and bought a few hundred dollars' worth of U.S. Savings Bonds and IBM stock,
determining that I would not touch those funds. When

Frank was old enough, he could decide for himself how he wanted to spend them.

As I began to provide for my son's physical needs, I also began to plan for his future in other ways. If I wanted him to join me in the ministry, I would have to share with him the vision God had given me—the vision of millions of souls going to hell and of God's holding me accountable for preaching to them. That meant not only telling him the details of the vision, but also letting him share the joys I was continuing to experience as more souls came to the Lord. He would have to see how much I needed workers to labor with me for the harvest of souls.

Of course, Frank would have to make up his own mind when he became old enough. I could not force him to live his life a certain way, nor could I tell him what vocation he had to choose. However, I intended to do everything spiritually possible to guide him toward the ministry, so that he would want to choose it.

As I had promised God, I did not intend to rear my son for the secular world. I would share the vision with him as clearly as I could, and once he comprehended it, I was certain his choice would be a natural one. I never really doubted that he—or the other children still to come—would follow me into the ministry.

From the beginning, I felt that my family would be an asset, not a liability to my ministry. When I married Louise Layman, I did not feel that I had picked up extra baggage and freight that I would have to drag after me. Instead, I was adding another engine to share in pulling that vision for souls into victorious reality. Also, my son—and the other children that would come after him—would add the second generation of laborers to the ministry.

Therefore, I began from Frank's birth to make a place for him in my life and ministry. As early as he could understand, I began to tell him about the joys of ministering and the great opportunities for him to follow and join me. He would grow up hearing that vision repeated over and over.

Three and a half years later, on June 27, 1950, our second son, Stephen, was born in South Bend, Indiana, where I had become pastor of the South Bend Gospel Tabernacle.

As I had done during the first pregnancy, I prayed daily over the second child as it was developing within the womb, asking God to bless the little one. When it came time for the delivery, I went with Louise to the hospital and was on hand to see my second son shortly after he was born.

The next day, which was still the first day of his life, I wrote this letter to Stephen:

Dearest Son,

At 11:47 P.M. (a Tuesday) you made your appearance in the great human world. You are welcome! We prayed for you and looked forward to your coming to live with us.

In the next few hours your mother and I will give you a name. You will wear it all the days of your life.

I saw you a few minutes after you were born and was thrilled to see your lovely body—you look very much like your brother Frank when he was a baby.

My son, I shall try to be the best father in the world, and I am hoping that you will make me a glad father—and that Christ shall be pleased with your life.

The world is in bad condition spiritually, morally, and politically. Three days before you were born, war broke out in Korea. But I want you to always be a real man and face every emergency of life with courage.

May God bless and keep you.

A letter from your daddy the first day of your life.

> With fatherly love,
> Lester Sumrall

By the time our third and last son was born, Louise and I and our two boys were living in the Philippines where I was in the midst of building a new church, Bethel Temple, in Manila. We had been praying for another child, and as I had done during both previous pregnancies, I prayed over the third child we were expecting. He arrived on October 17, 1953.

Carrying on the tradition I had begun with Frank, I wrote the following letter to my newborn third son:

To my third son:

My dear little son, you are just two hours old now.

Your father has just arrived back from the Mary Johnson Hospital where you were born. You and your precious mother are getting along fine. I am so happy for it.

This is your first night in this great new world. Unlike your two older brothers, Frank and Stephen, you were not born in your home country. You are born in a land where you are a stranger. I was standing surrounded by Chinese and Filipino people as you were wheeled by me from the delivery room. This will speak to you of the fact that we are of a truth pilgrims and strangers in the earth—our eternal home is heaven.

My dear son, I shall strive to be a good father to you. To the very best of my ability I shall seek to rear you in the way the Lord Jesus would have us. Your interest will always be near my heart. Until the day and hour, if the Lord tarries, that I am sure you are born again and determined to live a Christian life, I shall pray for your salvation. After your conversion, I shall continue to pray for the guidance of our Lord and Master in your life.

You will possibly be named Peter, and if so, I trust—like the great apostle of old—you will be fearless and determined to excel in the things of God. And I trust and pray that the faith of the great Apostle will be found in you also.

God bless you, dear little one. You have been born into a tempestuous world, torn asunder by war and misunderstanding. If Jesus tarries, may you help this poor world, in your small way, back to God.

Your loving father,
Lester Sumrall

In addition to the letters, I provided both my second and third sons the same gift that I had given to the first. After each was born, I went to the stockbroker and purchased a few hundred dollars' worth of IBM stock in their names. From the moment they were born, I gave each of them equal treatment.

To me, the purchase of stock was a gesture of love to my boys. I was not a rich man (although the Lord had allowed my ministry to prosper and had provided for us financially so that we never had to be in want), so the amount of stock I bought was never over a few hundred dollars. I did not purchase it for security, nor as insurance for the future. After all, we were depending upon Jesus for our futures. I was confident the stock would grow in value over the years as the boys grew, and that someday they would be able to use it for some special purchase.

I had chosen IBM because I believed the future of intricate office equipment was good. I also hoped that as the boys grew up and became aware of their nest egg, they would also come to appreciate the value of money and investment.

As it has turned out, now that all my sons are grown and have families of their own, they still own most of the stock I purchased for them when they were babies. Over the years, the stock has split a number of times and has grown in value.

Frank was able to take a portion of his stock investment and convert it into cash for the down payment on his home. Stephen bought a car with some of his stock. So far, Peter continues to hold on to all of his.

The practice of making investments for my sons was so successful that we are continuing it with our grandchildren. As each grandchild is born, Louise and I invest a small amount of stock in that child's name—still in amounts under a thousand dollars. We are confident that someday the stock will increase in value for them, too, and they will also come to appreciate the fact that their grandparents have cared for them very deeply. Regardless of whether the grandchild is a boy or a girl, we treat each one equally by buying each child an equal stock investment.

Such has been my commitment—not only to my sons, but also to my grandchildren. I have viewed them all as blessed gifts from the Lord—gifts for me to rear, to love, to teach, to guide, and to encourage into the ministry alongside me. I have respected them, even from their birth, and have had faith that they would develop into adults with ability and integrity. I have had faith in their future, because I began to put my future into them.

It was not until recently that I thought of putting all of this information—including the letters to my newborn sons—into a book. Although the way one rears his family is a very private business, there are millions of girls and boys who need direction in this area. Consequently, they and their parents might benefit from some of the ways

God has guided Louise and me in bringing up our own children.

I pray that other parents will become as committed to their children and grandchildren as we are to ours. I heartily recommend some kind of savings account be started for each newborn child. Who knows what benefits may accrue by the time that child is old enough to use it?

3

A House Full of Love

I love my family.

But more important than the fact that I *know* I love my family, or that I write about loving my family, is the need for my family to experience my love. A family needs to be built on love. It is the single most important ingredient in cementing family relationships.

Perhaps because Louise and I waited a long time before we married, we were more settled and mature in our love than we would have been if we had married as teenagers. By being older, we had developed a healthy faith in God—a faith that had experienced His miraculous love and grace. We knew that God's sacrificial love becomes the basis of love in a Christian's life, and we were constantly aware of His loving presence working in us.

When Louise and I were married on September 30, 1944, we brought with us a vast storehouse of love—a love poured into our hearts by the Holy Spirit. That love strengthened us and encouraged us, enabling us to serve God enthusiastically on the mission field. We had both seen God work wonders in transforming lives as we preached and ministered to people who had never before heard the gospel. The joy of seeing lives saved and brought into submission to Jesus Christ and empowered by the Holy Spirit is one of the ways God uses to assure us of His loving presence.

In fact, Louise was so conscientious about carrying out the ministry to which God had called her that before she accepted my proposal of marriage, she asked me, "Lester, what am I to do then with my calling to Argentina?"

"You'll have an even bigger calling," I replied. "We're going to minister to the whole world!"

Immediately after the wedding, we embarked on a two-year, fifty-thousand-mile honeymoon that saw us preaching and singing our way throughout the United States and Canada, and down into the Caribbean and South America. We loved it, and we loved each other. Often in Latin America, Louise had to interpret for me as I preached because I did not know the language there. She played the accordion and sang, either in Spanish or Portuguese as the congregation required. In our private devotions during those two years we read through the Bible together, from Genesis to Revelation.

To us, love was more than romantic attachment. From the beginning, we were committed to each other. We wanted each other. We had made a place in our lives for each other. We were also determined to make each other happy, no matter what the circumstances. Perhaps that is why in forty years of marriage so far, we have not had a single argument. (That does not mean we have had no disagreements, but we have always been able to discuss those disagreements in love and in a willingness to see the matter from the other's point of view.)

Having each of our children was a planned, loving act. Before each of them was conceived, Louise and I prayed together for a child, asking God to give us a boy or a girl that would grow up to serve Him and become a part of our ministry. Each child was wanted! None of our sons came to us by accident. We prayed for, longed for, and looked forward to the birth of each one.

Love for a child comes naturally when the child is conceived in such an atmosphere.

Some people say parents should have their children while they are "still young enough to enjoy them." Well, Louise and I have never known age to be a barrier to the enjoyment of our children. I think it all depends on how much you want children in the first place. I loved my children even before they were born! So it was only natural for me to continue loving them—and loving them even more—after they were born.

When the boys were little, I often came home after preaching or spending a tiring day on church business, and I still enjoyed getting down on the floor with my sons and rolling around and playing with them. I liked giving them my attention. I also gave them the best toys I could find, and whenever I went on a trip, I always brought back some gift for each of them—something I knew they would like, such as a T-shirt with the name of the city where I had been. At other times, I would get them all dressed up, and we would take them out to a nice restaurant.

I think my actions spoke for themselves. The boys knew I loved them. I also verbalized that love. I never considered it a lack of manliness to say, "I love you, Frank.... I love you, Steve.... I love you, Peter."

In fact, now that my sons are all grown men with families of their own, I still tell them aloud that I love them— and I do it frequently.

You see, my sons hold a preferred position in my thoughts at all times. After all, it was my purpose all along to rear them for Jesus!

I loved my family so much that I could not enjoy going

off on an extended tour without taking all of them with me. As a missionary and an evangelist, I moved around quite a bit while my sons were still young. Because of that transience, Frank was born in Springfield, Missouri; Stephen was born in South Bend, Indiana; and Peter was born in Manila, the Philippines. Of course, those were places where we settled into missionary work for several years at a time, and one would expect to take his family along. I also took mine on shorter tours—even though I didn't have to. One of those times was in 1956 when I felt the call of God to go to Israel for six months. I took the whole family along because I wanted them with me. I wanted them to be fully a part of everything I was doing.

Later we spent over two years in Hong Kong and afterward, two more years in the Philippines before the Lord settled us permanently in South Bend.

Everywhere we went, I was always careful to explain to the boys exactly why we were going, what I felt the Lord was calling me to do there, and what I believed He expected me to accomplish. My sons always felt they were an important part of my ministry. Although some missionaries go off and leave their families for two and three years at a time while they work on the mission field, I always assured my family that they were an integral part of my life overseas.

My son Frank still remembers traveling with us on an ocean freighter to the Philippines in 1952. He was only five years old, yet my explanation of why we were making the journey is still clear in his mind. He knew God had called me to leave our church in South Bend in order to build a new church in Manila. He remembers that the freighter was tossed about so badly in a typhoon that almost everyone on the ship became seasick. Frank and I did not. We got to eat more food that way, he says.

Our boys were showered with love, not only by Louise and me but also by the people in our congregations. In Manila, for instance, the Filipino people loved them so much they kept bringing them presents.

In the Philippines it was the custom to have local girls come in to do such things as the washing, cooking, and cleaning, and we hired them from our congregation. They became like members of the family, and in no time they were insisting on giving Peter his early-morning bottle so that Louise would not have to get out of bed. When we left Manila to return to South Bend, those girls were so upset at our leaving that they went with us to the airport, crying and taking turns holding little Peter for one last time.

In addition to taking my family with me everywhere in my travels, I also gave the boys free access to me regardless of where I was or what I was doing. When I was the pastor of a church and was in my office, the door was always open to my sons. I never pushed them aside. Instead, I wanted to help them and be available to them as much as I could. I never told them to be quiet and sit in the corner, or to leave the room because I was too busy with more important matters. If one of them had a problem, he could come in to see me, and I would put everything else aside and discuss it with him on the spot. My boys knew that the family took priority over work in the office.

Interestingly enough, none of my sons took advantage of this open-office policy. They did not try to monopolize my time. It seems that they understood the importance of what I was doing, and they left me alone to do it. They also understood that my work was never too important for me to spend time with them.

As the boys grew, I began to teach them various sports.

When each of them became five or six years of age, I took him out to a swimming pool and taught him how to swim. In the years when the boys were youngsters, we lived near a number of beaches, such as in Manila and Hong Kong. In those years, we spent a lot of time swimming. That was an excellent way for us to be together as a family.

I also taught the boys to play softball and basketball. After we settled down in South Bend, I also taught them how to play golf. We still all go out golfing regularly. Even today they find their dad a hard man to beat. As in all my activities, when I play golf, I play to win.

I was their coach, too. I always encouraged them in athletics when they were young, although I usually did not permit them to participate in the more dangerous sports, such as boxing and football. Participation in outdoor games gave them winning attitudes as well as a willingness to accept defeat graciously. It helped them to learn cooperation and coordination. It also toughened them up physically in preparation for the spiritual battles I knew they would have to fight in years to come.

I remember once when Frank was playing softball. He fell down and scraped his arm, and he came running to me, crying. I could see it was only a very minor scrape, and I knew the pain would soon go away.

"You're all right, son," I told him. "Go right back in there and show them how to play."

"But it hurts, Daddy."

"I know, but you're a big boy now. You can take it. You're not weak. You're strong."

Frank did go right back into the game, and he played harder than ever. He got the message.

I look back on those times with fondness: swimming

with my family in Manila Bay and playing softball on the grass along the beach; swimming in the China Sea at Hong Kong during the day and playing games at home in the evening (during the time I was building New Life Temple church); eating our lunches beside the ancient ruins at Caesarea and Sidon while I did research in the Jesus Library of the YMCA in Israel.

In South Bend we cut the grass together in our ten-acre yard. It was a big job, but it provided us a togetherness in purpose as well as in presence.

That kind of love and attention was bound to have some effect on our sons. Because they received our love and never were denied it, they were able to give their own love more freely to one another. My sons were not only brothers—they became one another's best friends as well.

Now I wouldn't be so naive as to say my sons never fought among themselves. They did. They were normal little boys, and there is a natural rivalry that develops amongs boys that expresses itself in wrestling, tussling, and other forms of competitiveness. But in our family it never got out of hand.

I think it was only after Peter was born that real rivalry showed up. Frank and Stephen had played together very well, with a minimum of fighting. They were only three and a half years apart in age. Then Peter came along, three and a half years after Stephen. When he became old enough to get in on the fun, he vied with Frank for Steve's companionship, and Frank didn't like it. That resulted in some fighting between Frank and the other two, and I had to warn him that since he was the eldest, he was expected to look out for his younger brothers. He was not to hit them. So it wasn't unusual for the two younger ones to pummel Frank while he gritted his teeth and took it. Yet I know there were times when Frank got in his licks too. At any rate, there was no serious violence, no vengeance, and no grudges.

The boys learned very early not to be selfish or to refuse to share their toys and other possessions with their brothers. Whenever there was any selfishness exhibited, I simply removed the disputed object and said, "See? Now nobody has it."

One way I discouraged selfishness was to treat all three boys alike. Whenever I bought one of them a toy or some other gift, I bought something for the two others as well. When the boys needed clothing, we took them all to the store and outfitted the three of them at the same time. I do not recall any real jealousy cropping up among my sons.

(Even today the boys continue to share things among themselves. For instance, Stephen has a swimming pool at his home, but he insists it belongs to us and to his brothers and their families as well. The pool is full a great deal of the time. I have even seen my sons buy suits for one another if they saw a need. There is a feeling of oneness among them that I find rare in families—especially American families—today.)

Out of this kind of family atmosphere, my sons developed a bond among themselves. I do not see any arrogance in them. I see a spirit of love and cooperation, of acceptance and common vision. I believe that if all Christian families stuck together as ours has, we could quickly win the world for Jesus. However, since such family unity is not widespread, the devil still has the upper hand over much of our country.

At this point I feel it is safe to say that between my life and those of my sons there has flowed human understanding and blessing. The boys do not have to overcome hostility and deprivation; they can launch out from a level of love and abundance that will enable them to help build God's kingdom from the point where I am now—not the point from which I started.

Today I am helping my sons to foster the same attitudes in their children. Frank's son, Lester, for instance, wanders into my office regularly. He calls me "Papa," and I keep a bag of candy in my desk drawer for him and the other grandchildren. I have not ever asked them to leave or told them that I am too busy to see them. Recently when I had a visitor in my office, Lester came in and asked me a couple of questions. Then he asked, "Do you want me to leave, Papa?"

"Well, that's up to you," I told him. "You don't have to."

He listened for a few minutes while the visitor and I talked, then he voluntarily left the room—perhaps to go see what his father was doing.

I treat my grandchildren the same as I treat my sons. When I hug them and kiss them, they say spontaneously, "You love me, don't you, Papa?"

And I say, "Yes, I do."

I treat all of my grandchildren as if they were my own sons and daughters. I make myself available to them, letting them know they are important to me.

The work of a missionary and television evangelist is demanding. I put in a lot of time and travel a lot of miles to preach the gospel. However, I also have to make time for my family.

They have top priority.

I love them all.

4

Training Up a Child

"Dad, I'm scared!"

I had heard the noise of someone rushing down the stairs to the kitchen in South Bend. In the doorway stood my youngest son, Peter, now fifteen. His face was deathly pale, and his eyes were wide.

"What's the matter, son?" I asked.

"In my room," he said haltingly, "the devil is in my room!"

"Peter," I responded, "if the devil is in your room, there has to be a reason. He doesn't come after Christians unless we've trespassed in his territory. What have you done?"

The color was coming back into his cheeks, but he hung his head and said, "A friend and I bought a Beatles record today. I know I wasn't supposed to, because you've said rock 'n' roll is of the devil. But I heard there are secret messages recorded on Beatles records, and you can hear them if you play the record backward."

"And you played it backward?" I asked.

"Yes. I took the record over to the church and taped it. Then I played the tape backward over the P.A. system."

I was not surprised. Peter is technologically inclined. He was always busy taking things apart and putting them back together. I had heard about the "back masking" on the Beatles and other records, and I understood the challenge to Peter's technological mind to figure out how it was done.

"But I didn't hear any words, Dad," Peter was saying. "There were just a lot of strange noises. It didn't make any sense at all."

I put my hand on Peter's shoulder.

"You did wrong, son," I said.

He nodded.

"Now you understand why I've said Christians must stay away from rock 'n' roll. It's part of the devil's playground."

"I know, Dad. I'm sorry."

"Well, we need to deal with the devil right now. Peter, I want you to pray and repent of what you've done."

He agreed, and told the Lord he was sorry for trespassing into the devil's territory.

Peter had learned his lesson, and I was thankful that he knew immediately what to do when he got into spiritual trouble. It was a testimony to the effectiveness of the spiritual guidance Louise and I had given to all of our boys from the moment they were born.

Putting my hand on Peter's head, I said, "Satan, you have no claim on my son! I command you in the name of Jesus to leave Peter and never to return or bother him again!"

Peter was visibly relieved.

"Go and sleep in our bedroom tonight," I told him. "I'm going up to your room and deal with that unclean spirit."

As soon as I entered Peter's room I was aware of the evil presence. It had not remained in the church. That territory was too holy for it, for it could not bear to stay in a place where the name of Jesus was mentioned so often. It had followed Peter home, thinking it might eventually get him under its power.

Standing in Peter's bedroom, I spoke strong words: "Unclean spirit, by the authority of Jesus Christ, and through the power of His blood, I command you to leave these premises! This house is dedicated to the Lord. You do not have permission to remain here. Go, and never return!"

I undressed and slept in Peter's bed that night. The evil presence was gone and never returned.

That strange episode is an illustration of the importance of training our children clearly in spiritual matters. There are many Christian parents today who see nothing wrong with rock 'n' roll, as long as their children like it and it keeps them occupied and entertained. However, if we live our lives close to the Lord, pray together as families and study the Bible together, we will see such evils much more clearly and be able to separate ourselves from these influences of Satan.

From the moment each of our sons was born, Louise and I considered his spiritual development as important as providing food for his physical body or making sure that he was warmly dressed. We had prayed for each child carefully before he was born, and now that he was in the world, we continued our diligent prayers for his welfare and eventual salvation.

Whenever any of our sons thinks back to his earliest memories of the spiritual climate in our home, he will remember either his mother or his father praying over him in bed at night. Also, as soon as he learned to talk, we taught him to pray as well. Then when he learned to read, we gave him his turn reading from the Bible during family devotions.

That spiritual emphasis was never forced, however. It

was always a pleasant, positive experience for our sons. It was a warm, happy time together with their parents and brothers.

Louise has told me that when Peter was a little boy, she was praying over him at bedtime, saying, "Lord, please bless my little lamb."

Peter looked up at her with a big smile and said in a loud voice, "Baa-a-a-a!"

His mother looked at him in surprise and asked, "Now what was that for?"

"Well, you said I was your little lamb," Peter replied.

You see, our relationship with God was a natural part of family life, not something extra that was forced on the boys at specific times of the day or the week. They learned very early who God was, who Jesus was, and who the Holy Spirit was. They learned who the devil was too. They knew that their mother and I were working for Jesus, and that the devil was our enemy, who would try to prevent those lost souls from turning their lives over to Jesus by keeping them blind to the truth.

When the boys were old enough to go to school, Louise and I prayed with them each morning at breakfast and read a short passage of Scripture. Then each evening after dinner, we all gathered in a circle in the living room for family devotions. For the next half hour to forty-five minutes we read the Bible, discussed what we had read, talked about the way God had been working in our lives. Then, one by one, we prayed aloud according to whatever was on our hearts. Prayer and Bible reading were such a natural part of our lives that the boys felt that anyone who did not pray or read the Bible was abnormal.

It was the same with going to church. Church was such a normal part of our boys' lives—from their earliest memories of the crib room and of Sunday school kindergarten—that there never was any question of not going to church. I never had to tell them they had to go to church. It was always understood that church was the place we were supposed to be—Sunday morning and evening, at the midweek service, and whenever there was anything else going on there. The boys did not even stay home from midweek services to study for important tests in school. Church always had priority in our lives.

I have always believed—and still do—that if we provide the proper Christian atmosphere for our children in the home and at church, we do not have to preach at them as parents in order to pressure them into making a commitment to Christ. As our sons prayed with us and read the Bible and attended regular church services, they were presented with the whole gospel—the sinfulness of the world and its separation from God, the need for repentance, salvation through the blood of Jesus Christ, and the baptism in the Holy Spirit. They heard it from their earliest memories, and the gospel became a part of their world.

Our eldest son, Frank, still remembers singing gospel songs on my radio program when he was only four years old. He remembers standing on the stairwell at home, saying to us downstairs, "Repent or perish!"

All of my sons sat in the front row at church (where I could keep an eye on them), and they were always a captive audience. However, I never put any pressure on them individually to make a personal commitment to Christ. They heard the same message that the rest of the congregation heard. I did tell each of them that the altar was always open for their responses and that they were free to go forward at any time, either for salvation or any other need.

Frank, in fact, was five years old when he sensed the

first real move of God on his life. It was a Sunday morning when we had a visiting missionary in the pulpit. During the worship service, Frank felt a strong desire to have the personal experience of salvation. As the missionary was speaking, Frank knew he wanted to give his heart totally to God. At the close of the service, when the invitation to the altar was given, Frank immediately went forward, tears streaming down his face. He was deeply moved, and he knew right then that he, too, wanted to be a preacher.

Our boys responded to the altar call scores of times when they were young. Speaking from his own experience, our second son Stephen has said, "Most missionary kids are saved sixty times before they grow up."

Stephen also responded to altar calls in his early years, but he feels the time he made his first real commitment to Christ was around the age of ten. (I baptized him in water when he was thirteen and in the eighth grade.)

Like his brother Stephen, our youngest son, Peter, made several trips to the altar. The first time he committed his life to Christ was at the age of five.

As with their salvation, I never pressured the boys to seek baptism in the Holy Spirit. It was simply a part of their training in our Bible studies, in their Sunday school classes, and in the sermons they heard. They were fully aware of what the Bible says in Acts 1 and 2, and in 1 Corinthians 12 and 14 about the Holy Spirit and the gifts of the Spirit.

So it did not surprise me one summer back in Indiana when Frank was eleven years old that he came home from youth camp and announced excitedly that he had received a mighty baptism in the Holy Spirit.

Stephen received his baptism in the Holy Spirit at a special youth retreat when he was about thirteen.

Peter was about the same age that Stephen had been when he and the rest of his youth group lined up after their meeting one day so that the leaders could lay hands on them. Peter, with other members of the youth group, was baptized in the Holy Spirit.

Of course, the boys continued to have spiritual experiences with God after their baptism in the Spirit. I encouraged reconsecration to the Lord, and it always made me feel good to see them respond.

All three boys developed good habits of personal devotions. They rose early and had a time with the Lord before coming to breakfast, and often I would ask them any insights they had gained from the Bible during their devotion.

Along with our attention to spiritual things, all of us sought to live according to God's standards of personal holiness. That meant no smoking, no drinking of alcoholic beverages, and no dancing. Neither were the boys allowed to go to private parties at which boys and girls could become overly familiar with one another.

We sent notes to school telling the teachers our boys were not permitted to take part in square dancing, even though it was being taught as part of their classes.

In addition, they were not permitted to go to the movies or listen to rock 'n' roll because of the sensuous and satanic influences there. My son Peter's experience with the Beatles record was proof of my assertion from the pulpit that such things are from the devil.

That does not mean my sons never transgressed in some of these areas. Frank also stepped out of bounds at times. As a teenager, he says he felt some peer pressure from some of the boys at school because he was a preacher's son. Several times he had to stand up and be counted for the Lord.

My Three Sons

In rearing my sons, I have endeavored to protect their destiny by giving them a solid foundation in the faith. In 1956, while I was in Israel with my family, the Lord spoke to me and told me I was responsible for taking a million souls to heaven. That is an awesome responsibility. If my own sons were not among that number, I would consider my ministry a failure.

Some parents are so lax with their children's spiritual lives that they do not insist on their going to church and Sunday school, nor do they pray together and read the Bible. Their children grow up like weeds, putting down roots in whatever soil happens to be convenient. If that soil does not happen to be the Christian religion, the parents say, "Well, we thought it best to allow them to choose for themselves." That should never be the response of a Christian parent who has a vital, living relationship with the Lord Jesus Christ. We need to nurture our children in the faith and pray for them daily in order that their souls will be saved and that they will practice a living faith in Christ.

Our family's attention to living our faith and spreading the gospel was so strong that we did not even take the kind of vacations most Americans take. We went to Christian evangelistic meetings, camp-meetings or spiritual retreats, where the gospel was central to the purpose of the trip.

In fact, in 1968 I had printed one million pamphlets in the three official languages of the Olympics. We drove to Mexico City to distribute them and to evangelize the people at the Olympic Games. It was a wonderful experience for the boys, who were enthusiastic about reaching people of all nations.

Yes, our family totally and fully enjoyed itself. We went swimming whenever possible, often in the swimming pool of a hotel or motel where we were staying during the meetings. We got plenty of exercise. But our great ambitions were toward the Lord. We were living for Him twenty-four hours a day.

When you and your family can live together like that, the devil doesn't have much of a chance.

5

Spare Not the Rod—Or the Belt

The popular old saying, "Spare the rod and spoil the child" is not very popular in our country any more. In Sweden, it is more than unpopular. There, spanking has been made illegal, and a parent can be arrested just for spanking his child.

But we will all be the losers if we continue to rear generations of undisciplined children. We will reap a harvest of rebellion that will spell the downfall of society.

As a Christian I have to believe that God knows what He is talking about when He says, "Do not withhold correction from a child, For if you beat him with a rod, he will not die. You shall beat him with a rod, and deliver his soul from hell" (Prov. 23:13–14).

I was determined from the beginning that my children would be obedient. Therefore, I was not reluctant to use physical punishment whenever I considered it necessary to provide the desired correction in my sons' behavior. Neither do I believe in the overuse of physical punishment, because that can result in child abuse. I believe in spanking only as a last resort. Usually, I simply gave my boys a good talking to.

My wife and I are orderly people. We lead disciplined lives, and we tried to instill that kind of self-discipline in our boys as well. We feel a Christian should use all of his time as efficiently and effectively as possible in serving God.

I am often out of bed by four o'clock in the morning making notes for my sermons or my teaching series or television programs. I work sixteen hours a day and more in the ministry, yet I never feel any strain or stress. I work like that only because I love what I am doing. I try to make every waking moment productive in some way because I do not want any loose motion in my life.

Now as I have already said, this does not mean that all I do is work because I spend a lot of time with my family too. Regardless of how busy I am, I will drop everything when one of my sons comes in to see me to spend time with him. You see, that relationship with my children is as important a part of my ministry as any other duties I perform. What I am doing, then, is using the time God has given me for purposes that will be the most productive in His kingdom.

Louise maintains an orderly house. Everything is clean and in place. The beds are made, and dinner is on the table on schedule. When the boys were small, I cannot remember a day when they were late getting ready for church. They would follow me over to the church building and trail me around while I checked to see that everything was in readiness for the service.

On the subject of discipline, my wife and I are one. We also exercised oneness in carrying out correction. If one of the boys misbehaved while I was not there, Louise would never tell them, "Wait until your father gets home." She would take care of the matter right then and there. If a spanking was needed, she administered it with a hairbrush or strap.

Now, I do not claim that we were perfect in the way we

disciplined our children. There were times when the boys felt we were unfair. Frank, for instance, got the most spankings. This was partly because he needed them, but it was also because he was our first child and as a new father, I tended to overcorrect at first.

I can still remember standing in front of the congregation one Sunday evening, dismayed at the way Frank was cutting up and acting silly on the front pew. Louise and I had both told him he was supposed to behave himself in church, but he had difficulty remembering. He was beginning to distract some of the congregation from the message I was preaching.

In the middle of the sermon I stopped, asked the congregation to sing a chorus, and went down to the pew and took Frank by the arm.

"Come with me," I said.

We walked into the back room behind the pulpit.

"Do you know why I brought you here?" I asked.

Tears were beginning to well up in Frank's eyes.

"Because I was being bad," he said.

"Well, what did I tell you to do?"

"Behave in church."

"And what were you doing?"

He shrugged his shoulders.

"Were you behaving the way I told you?"

He shook his head.

"And what did I tell you would happen if you didn't behave in church?" I asked.

"Get a spanking."

"Do you deserve a spanking?"

Reluctantly he nodded.

I gave him his spanking; then, as I could hear the congregation going into the third repetition of the chorus, I held him in front of me and asked, "Now do you think you can behave for the rest of the service?"

He nodded, drying his tears. I hugged him.

"I love you, Frank," I said.

"I know. I love you, too, Daddy."

I walked him back to his seat, then resumed my sermon. Frank sat like a little gentleman for the rest of the service.

I always made sure my sons knew why they were being punished. We had rules in our home, rules for proper behavior in church and rules for behavior away from home. They were consistent, and I always told the boys clearly what I expected of them. When they disobeyed, they knew they would get a spanking—no matter where we were. If we happened to be in a restaurant, I would take the guilty one off to the men's room and administer punishment there before returning him to his seat at the table. The punishment immediately followed the infraction. I never told them, "You're going to get it when you get home."

My usual means of spanking was to use my belt. It was always handy and it was always effective.

One of the things I guarded against was punishing them in anger. The only times I have delayed punishment were the times when my sons made me angry. Then I waited until I was certain there was no anger in me that would cause me to mistreat them during punishment.

I always talked to my boys first before punishing them. We discussed what they had done wrong and why it was wrong, and we made sure they had been aware beforehand that it was wrong. If necessary, I even opened the Bible and read about the particular offense they had committed or about the need for children to be corrected. Then together we knelt and prayed as they confessed their wrongdoing. Often the tears began right there. Afterward, I would take my belt, tell them to bend over (I never wrestled them into position), and hit them a couple of times—just hard enough that it hurt, but not hard enough to injure them.

Afterward, I always made sure to hug them, kiss them, and assure them that I loved them.

I believe that form of punishment is consistent with the Bible's instruction to parents on the way to correct children, and I believe my sons realized that I was being consistent with what God wanted. None of them ever resented being punished. They all agree today it was for their good.

Fairness and understanding must be given priority in parent-child relationships. That is particularly important when it comes to discipline. If a father speaks as an autocrat and does not permit his children, wife, or others to speak or to answer him, he separates himself from their fellowship. If he screams at them or speaks out of anger, he loses their love, respect, faithfulness—and his cause. I constantly explained the importance of our work for the Lord and the reasons we had to work together as a family.

In temperament, my second son, Stephen, has always been the opposite of his brothers. When he chose to be, he was introverted and obedient. We did not have to spank him very much. Sometimes if we even raised our voices to him he began to cry. Steve has his mother's quiet, reserved nature, while Frank is more outgoing and energetic, as I am.

If Frank has my nature and Stephen is more like his mother, then Peter, our youngest, lies somewhere between the two. Many times I have had to tell him to settle down.

I found that as the boys grew into their teens, they needed a lot more counseling with each punishment.

They were reaching an age when physical punishment loses its effectiveness. (In fact, many disciplinarians say physical punishment is effective only until about the age of twelve or thirteen. I spanked my sons when they were older than that, but only for serious transgressions.) Gradually I phased out the spankings in favor of talking man-to-man. Usually those counseling sessions, coupled with a denial of privileges, were sufficient discipline to bring their behavior back into line.

To some people in American society today, corporal punishment sounds harsh. It isn't. I believe it is quicker and a lot more effective than many other forms of punishment used by parents nowadays. Punishment that involves rejection of the child or that humiliates him becomes a form of mental cruelty that can result in emotional problems later in the child's life.

My sons have grown up disciplined, healthy in mind and body, and with strong, positive attitudes about life and their place in the world. Moreover, they are fine Christian men, which I think is a testimony itself to the effectiveness of God's way to discipline children.

6

A Moral Foundation

One of the aspects of my sons' lives that I have guarded most carefully is their moral integrity.

From the moment each of my sons was born, I began making plans for him to follow me into the ministry and to catch the vision God had given me for rescuing souls from hell. Therefore, it was important both to them and to me that they lead clean lives and not bring any reproach upon Christ or upon the ministry. I have seen too many pastors and evangelists fall into the sin-breeding traps of the devil. Once a minister falls morally, he loses his integrity, his leadership, and eventually his ministry. I was determined to do all I could to ensure nothing like that happened to my sons.

At home, our teaching on morals grew out of our regular family devotions. Everything we need to know about truthfulness, honesty, and sexual purity is contained in the Bible. We studied the Ten Commandments and the Sermon on the Mount, so that there would be no doubt in our boys' minds when they were faced with moral choices.

I suppose I was severest in punishing my sons for lying, because that was the sin they were most likely to commit. Once when they were all still quite young, they were playing softball outside the house. Frank hit the ball through one of the windows. He knew he was going to be punished for it, so he talked it over with his two younger brothers. They all agreed not to tell who had broken the window. When I called them in, they stood in a row in front of me, shuffling their feet and looking back and forth at one another.

"How did the window get broken?" I asked.

They all shrugged their shoulders.

"Well, now, one of you had to have done it. Which one was it?"

They looked at the floor, shuffled some more and shrugged their shoulders. It was so comical—they appeared to have rehearsed their performance for a stage production.

"Does any one of you know who did it?"

They all shook their heads.

"Frank, what do you suppose the punishment should be for breaking the window?"

"A spanking, I guess," he said.

"Do the rest of you agree?"

They all nodded again.

"Well, I'll tell you what I'm going to have to do, boys. Since I know one of you broke the window, but none of you seems to know who it was, I'll have to spank all three of you. After all, you've just told me a lie in saying you don't know who did it. Does one of you wish to confess now?"

They looked at one another again, but no one offered to accept the blame. So I kept my word and spanked all three of them.

The boys learned truthfulness clearly from their parents. Louise and I had no reason to lie, but once in Hong Kong the boys thought that we just might possibly be hiding some unbiblical behavior from them. They had some Swedish friends at the public school they were attending, and the Swedish friends found it incredible when our boys told them that Louise and I did not smoke. I guess those other boys had never known an adult who did not smoke. Anyway, our sons asked us about it.

"Why, boys, you know that I preach against smoking," I said. "How could your mother and I do something I preach against?"

"Well, Dad, some boys in school told us that everybody smokes," Frank said.

"Who were they?"

"Oh, some boys from Sweden. They said you and Mom probably do it in private so that we don't find out about it."

Louise and I were both amused by the Swedish boys' reasoning. It gave us a good opportunity to open the Bible with our sons again and review its teachings about the body being the temple of the Holy Spirit (see 1 Cor. 6:19). It said we were not to defile God's temple with anything that is sinful or not good for it.

"If I were to preach one thing but practice just the opposite, I would be a hypocrite and a liar, wouldn't I, boys?" I said.

They got the point. We need to be truthful in our actions as well as in our words.

When it came to teaching my sons about sexuality, I knew there was a lot more involved than a simple "This is right" and "That is wrong" approach. Sexuality involves our total relationship to those of the opposite sex—and in a way, to those of the same sex as well. In addition to right and wrong, I wanted my sons to know about respect and responsibility.

The Bible has some definite words about sexual relationships, such as, "You shall not commit adultery" (Ex. 20:14), "Now the body is not for sexual immorality" (1 Cor. 6:13), and "You shall not lie with a male, as with a woman. It is an abomination" (Lev. 18:22). I wanted my sons not only to know those as maxims but also to know about temptations and dealing with the lusts of the flesh.

As each boy reached the age when I felt it was time to discuss sexuality, I took him aside and explained as fully as I could the functions of the male and female bodies, and the purpose for which God had created them. I made it clear that sexual relationships were not dirty, but were holy and pure when they were entered into within the context of marriage. I taught them about their responsibilities toward girls—that they were as responsible as the girls were to maintain the purity of their relationships.

I taught them about homosexuality and the danger that homosexuals might try to make advances toward them. I am fully aware that Satan is out to corrupt those in the ministry, including their families, and I did not want them to be ignorant of any of his wiles.

Fortunately my sons were always surrounded by clean-living Christian men and women after whom they could model their behavior and the behavior of girls they would meet and date. In our home they constantly had to relate to women: their mother, their grandmother (my mother), and their aunt (my sister), whose husband, Reverend James Murphy, serves with me in the ministry. They learned a healthy respect for women in the home. I encouraged them to carry that respect over into relationships with women outside the home.

One of my most important pieces of advice on dating was that they should be very selective in the choice of any girl they wanted to take out. To me, dating is not just a boy and girl going out to have a good time with no

Louise and I with Frank, our first son, in the parsonage of my first pastorate, in South Bend (1949).

Our family at Christmas. Frank was now 4; Stephen was 1 (1950).

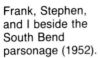
Frank, Stephen, and I beside the South Bend parsonage (1952).

Louise reading to the boys (1952).

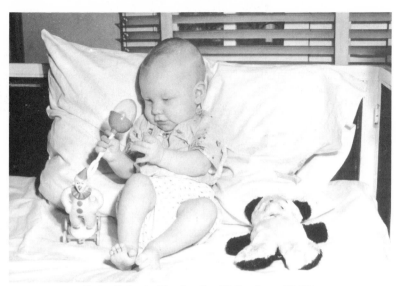

Baby Peter in Manila, the Philippines (1953).

Frank and Stephen at the
Bible school campus where
we lived in Manila (1954).

This picture was taken just before our Hong Kong ministry (1959).

Our family with a missionary friend in Hong Kong (1962).

This picture was taken at Manila Bethel Temple during our second term in that city (1962).

Here, in Manila, we are wearing Filipino-style dress and shirts (1965).

Frank and Stephen play an instrumental duet in Manila Bethel Temple (1965).

Frank relaxes by playing basketball in Manila (1965).

A family songfest shortly after we returned from the Philippines (1966).

Frank and I in my church office in South Bend (1970).

(left to right) Frank, myself, Peter, and Stephen at Peter's wedding (Sept. 18, 1976).

thought that the relationship might lead to something more serious or permanent. I told my boys they should not date any girl they would not want to spend the rest of their lives with. I also told them to look carefully at the girl's mother because it was quite likely that someday the girl would look and behave much the way her mother does today.

I encouraged our sons to date only Christian girls. I explained to them that with a girl outside the church, their different faiths would become a sore point of disagreement. This could affect their own relationship with God. (King Solomon, for instance, sinned and brought idol worship back into the kingdom of Israel by intermarrying with pagan women.) I told them that their relationship with God and their service to Him had to be overriding factors for them to consider.

As it turned out, the boys never were attracted to any girls who were not Christians. As teenagers living at home, they always asked permission to take a girl out, and they abided by my rule that they be home by ten or eleven o'clock.

Since our boys went to public high schools, I felt there might be temptations to date girls there—even nonchristian girls—but that never happened.

Abraham in the Old Testament was the kind of father I wanted to be. He was so concerned for the welfare of his son Isaac that he would not allow him to marry one of the Canaanite women. Instead, he sent one of his servants to the land of Abraham's relatives in order to find a woman of their own kind for Isaac to marry. Genesis 24 details how God guided the servant to Rebekah, granddaughter of Abraham's brother, Nahor.

I wanted to be that concerned for my own sons. I urged them to marry only Christian girls, knowing that the women they chose as their wives would be an important part of their future ministry.

My instructions to my sons regarding the danger of homosexual advances was instruction time well spent. Homosexuals have become much more brazen in recent years, and I wanted my boys to have no doubts about how to deal with them.

Because morals are so important to the Christian, especially a Christian in or going into the ministry, I have sought to guard my sons and my home from temptation.

When our sons were small, I was reluctant to allow them to spend the night at a friend's house unless that family was strongly Christian. And even then, I had to be sure the boys would sleep in separate beds so that no unnecessary temptation might be aroused out of curiosity.

Today many families try to protect their homes from intruders who would break in and steal their valuable material possessions. They even put up chain-link fences and install burglar alarms. But we also have to be careful to guard our homes against the more insidious kinds of intrusions—the sins that Satan would use to entrap us.

If a person is morally corrupt, especially involving sexual sins, he will attempt to find a partner, no matter where he is. He might even be one of your own relatives visiting in your home. Therefore, I have been careful about whom I have allowed to stay under my roof—no matter how close a relative he might be. I wanted to make sure that I did not give the devil a chance with my family. Incest has destroyed a number of fine Christian homes. So I teach that we need to be careful about our relatives, particularly cousins, in-laws, aunts, uncles, stepfathers, stepmothers, stepbrothers, and stepsisters.

All of my sons are now married and rearing families of their own. Frank married a girl from London, Ontario,

Canada, and they have a son named Lester Leonard Sumrall.

Steve waited until he was twenty-eight before marrying. His wife, Diane, was a member of our congregation. Although he had dated a couple of other girls before, Diane was the first one he was serious about. They now have two little girls, Rachelle and Leslie.

Peter, too, married a girl from our congregation. However, before he made the final decision to get married, he came to me for a long talk about his responsibilities as a husband and father. He and his wife, Sue, now have two sons, David and Andrew, and a daughter, Angela.

Because all of my sons are involved with me in the ministry in one way or another, I always have them and their families around me. We are a happy, compatible family, frequently gathering for family meals.

We seek to be a clean-living family. I thank God that He gave me the foresight to plan for and train up my children to fulfill their roles properly, without getting into serious trouble along the way.

Today, with our nation in such moral disgrace, I am able to stand before God and say, "Here, I have brought up my children as You have instructed. Now they are Yours."

7

The Value of Money

It is very important that children learn the value of money at an early age. If my sons were to follow me in the ministry, they needed to learn how to handle money as carefully as I did.

There were various ways they learned the value of money. One was in understanding how I handled it—and why. They learned from my example, and they learned my philosophy about the use of earthly goods.

Back in chapter 2 of this book, I mentioned that at the birth of each of my sons, I invested a few hundred dollars in stocks and bonds, which I felt would grow in value as the boys grew. I believe in investing money in order to get a good return on it. However, the investments were always just a little something extra, not something I depended on for security.

God has always provided for us whenever we were building a new church or starting a new ministry. He has continued to provide for us abundantly through the years. We have never had to do without, although there have been times when cash got a little tight in our home.

I believe God has blessed me materially in my ministry because I have kept myself sanctified and have never used the profits for myself. As missionaries, Louise and I learned to live on a limited income. I have never allowed myself to become so concerned about money that it contaminated me or became a kind of security. In whatever ministry God has allowed me to serve, I have always kept only enough of the income to provide my family the necessities of life. The rest of the money has gone into the ministry, whether for building a new church or starting and expanding my radio and television ministry.

Because of this attitude toward money, great prosperity has followed me in all of my missionary and evangelistic ministries. The churches I have built, both overseas and in South Bend, have grown in value, attendance, and influence. Everywhere in the world that God has placed me, the ministry has flourished, economically and spiritually.

In South Bend, where we have the headquarters of the Lester Sumrall Evangelistic Association, Inc. (LESEA, Inc.), we have a church, a Bible school, and a publishing ministry. In addition, in South Bend and Indianapolis we own two television stations. All this was built from nothing, and today it is of great worth. Yet I own none of it personally. It is all in a not-for-profit corporation in which the investment is used exclusively to broadcast the gospel and to win souls to Christ.

Today when I travel and speak as an evangelist and Bible teacher, I often return to South Bend with offerings of several thousand dollars. This money goes into the world outreach ministry.

I have always wanted my sons to have this same attitude toward money. Therefore, I have always been open with them in letting them know what I was doing with the Lord's money.

When we were living in Hong Kong, for instance, I told them about my practice of loaning out my paychecks and getting twelve percent annual interest. It was completely businesslike, through one of the Hong Kong banks, and was a protected investment. Each time I received my check, I took it to the bank. But instead of just cashing the check and putting the money into my checking account, I used it to purchase one of the bank's investment checks, which was postdated for sixty days in the future. The face value of the check included two months' worth of interest at the twelve percent annual rate.

At the end of sixty days I cashed the check and had just a little more money than I had received from my missionary salary. It was not a lot of money, of course, but I figured I had put the Lord's money to good use.

I have the same philosophy in the use of time. I feel that I have to make the best use possible of my hours, days, and weeks, using that time for the Lord. Therefore, I am just as careful to see that the Lord's money is used profitably, getting as high a return as possible in order to plow it back into the ministry and build God's kingdom.

Many times, as a way of saving money, the men of our church and I would do whatever labor we could in building a new church. It was not unusual for me to join the elders and deacons in digging holes for footings and pouring concrete in order to economize on construction costs.

Those were the things my sons saw me doing   also had some other, more practical ways of teaching them the value of money. One was not to give them automatic allowances.

I believe that if parents buy their children everything they want or give them allowances as a hand-out, children find it difficult to learn anything about handling their own money properly. It simply spoils the children. They come to expect the money each week, although they have done nothing to merit it.

Therefore, our boys had to earn their money. However, they earned it at home. The jobs were not major or difficult. We assigned a value to chores such as cleaning up their rooms, making their beds, drying dishes, taking out the garbage, bringing in wood, mowing the grass, and any other little jobs that boys might be expected to do.

Besides paying our sons for working, we opened savings accounts for each of them. Each week they were told to put a portion of their earnings into their accounts. From the time each boy was twelve years old, he had his own account and could see the balance building up. He could spend part of his money on little things he wanted right away, but there was always that reserve that could be used for larger purchases he might want later on.

We allowed the boys to spend the money as they wanted, but we did counsel them in spending it wisely. I sometimes dissuaded them from purchases I considered foolish, but for the most part they exercised their own control over their accounts.

They did make mistakes, of course. I felt they had to. It was the best way they could learn to handle their own money. For instance, one week Frank spent most of the money he'd earned that week to buy a toy "water rocket." It seemed like a marvelous piece of equipment to him, and he was eager to show it off to his brothers and his friends.

But after he had launched the rocket only a couple of times that day, it landed hard on the pavement of the church parking lot and broke into several pieces. It could not be fixed.

"Oh, no!" he cried. "After all the money I spent on it! I had to work almost a week to get it, and now it's broken!"

It was a hard lesson for Frank, but it taught him the value of weighing the importance of his purchases and checking the quality of the merchandise.

Of course, there were many things the boys wanted to buy that cost more than they could afford, even after saving up their home-earned income. Whenever we deemed such purchases desirable, we bought the things for them ourselves, emphasizing that they were gifts of love from their mother and me. But we never allowed them to think we would buy them everything they wanted.

We also taught them to be careful about taking care of their clothing, so that the garments would last as long as possible. When some item of clothing was damaged, we repaired it rather than replacing it. We emphasized that clothing is a major expense, and that replacing torn clothing with something new is not always possible.

Each of our sons also learned that he had a greater responsibility with his money than simply spending it wisely. Money still was the Lord's money, and God had first claim on it. In the Bible, the Israelites gave the first 10 percent of their agrarian income, whether from the harvest of their fields or the increase in their herds, as an offering to the Lord. God has always blessed His people who tithe faithfully, giving Him back the first 10 percent of their own income. I have practiced tithing all my Christian life, and I taught my sons that I expected no less of them.

I always encouraged my sons to work at jobs that helped the ministry. There were plenty of jobs to do around the home and the church, so they did not have to go anywhere else to earn money.

One day, for instance, Peter came to me when he was about thirteen or fourteen and said he wanted to get a part-time job at a hamburger stand down the street from our church in South Bend.

"Are you sure that's what you want to do?" I asked him.

"Well, I thought it would be a good experience for me,

and I want to earn some extra money."

"But that would take you away from the church, and there's such a lot to do around here," I said.

"I was thinking about the pay...."

"I'll tell you what, son. There is more than enough to do at the church that will keep you busy for a long time to come. The fountain at the entrance, for instance, needs to be cleaned out. It looks pretty bad. You go to work on that, and I'll pay you fifteen cents an hour more than you could earn at the hamburger place. Is that fair?"

Peter's face suddenly brightened.

"Yes, sir! I'll start on it tomorrow!"

"Good boy."

I hugged him and sent him off, both of us happy in the knowledge that Peter would be doing something useful at the church. He was pleased as could be that he would be making more money doing that than he could earn someplace else.

I gave my sons many jobs to do around the church, but they never received preferential treatment in terms of duties or pay. They started at the bottom, doing the most menial janitorial chores. I can still picture Peter, his pants rolled up to his knees, wading in the church fountain and scrubbing out the algae and dirt.

I realize that not all parents can hire their own children that way and pay them more money than they could earn at a fast-food restaurant, but I strongly recommend ensuring that our children work in places that support their spiritual commitment. When a boy or girl wants to go to work for the first time, I believe it is imperative that the parents check out the atmosphere of the workplace and meet the manager. It could go a long way toward avoiding an unpleasant experience with bad language and other vices.

A further teaching to my sons on the value of money was my advice not to buy on credit. They learned this from my example first. If we could not pay cash in our family, we did not buy. To me, buying on credit and then having to pay interest is like paying for a dead horse. You cannot feed it or use it; it is just dead.

So no matter what the purchase was, whether furniture or new clothes, we always paid cash, and I advised my sons always to pay cash as well. If they had any doubts, even after they were grown and earning their own money, I told them I was always available to help them decide on their purchases so they could stay within their cash budget. I often went with them to compare prices and quality, and to negotiate a lower price if possible.

Steve is careful about his use of credit. He has a limited number of credit cards and uses them sparingly. He believes that the wise use of credit can be a benefit. He is managing his own money, as well as the affairs of the LESEA ministry, admirably.

Peter was so conscientious about avoiding credit that, when he got married, he lived in his home for a year without living room furniture until he and Sue could save up enough money to pay cash.

As our boys were growing up, there came a time when each of them was ready to have his own car. That, too, was operated on a cash basis.

Today, all of my sons are married and working in the ministry, and know how to handle not only their own money but the ministry's money as well. I once had to show them how to negotiate for major purchases, but today they do the negotiating for me.

Peter alone, as general manger of the television stations, negotiated the purchase of a $230,000 earth station for a satellite hookup. He also led in negotiating a $2.5

million-dollar contract with a major manufacturer of television equipment.

Stephen, meanwhile, is in charge of managing the LESEA organization, which includes managing our money. He, too, is a good negotiator and has been responsible for acquiring hundreds of thousands of dollars' worth of office equipment, including computers and printing equipment.

All of my sons understand the responsibility we have to the Lord and to our donors, for all of the money we receive comes from the tithes and gifts of Christians. Any expansion of our ministry is preceded by a lot of prayer and discussion. We make certain that we have the mind of the Lord on the way we are to go. Then we know He will provide. We never just assume the money will keep coming in, or build new facilities based on "projected donations," as some other ministries have done and suffered severe financial difficulties as a result.

Because of their training in managing money, my sons have a good business sense, which is something the Lord can use to continue to build a solid ministry. I am satisfied that the teaching I gave them has produced conservative Christian businessmen as well as good ministers of the gospel of Jesus Christ.

8

Being Careful about Friendships

As much attention as parents give their children, there are still many other influences that come into young lives that can either draw them closer to the kingdom of God or lure them away from it. Peer pressure is a powerful factor that must be considered by any Christian parent.

Louise and I decided early that if we were to rear our children successfully for the kingdom of God, we needed to pay special attention to the friends our sons made. The first thing we felt we had to do was provide the proper environment in which they could make the right kind of friends—in church, in the neighborhood, and in the schools they attended. Ninety-nine percent of a child's friends are made in those three environments.

Our lives were wrapped up in the church, of course, and in all kinds of evangelistic and missionary endeavors. The boys were with us in church three and four times a week. There they met, played with, and became friends with children from other Christian families. I believe a child's primary friends should come from families within the church.

A pastor has an advantage in steering his children toward friendships in the church because he is responsible for the kind of church they are in. He and his family are naturally around the church a great deal of time. For other families, I always advise them that they must be very careful to select the proper church in which to worship. Their children will be influenced not only by what they learn in Sunday school and in the worship services but also by the friends they make among their own peer groups. Children often develop lifelong friendships in the church, and the impressions they receive from the behavior of these friends can affect their social relationships for years to come—perhaps for life.

Our boys had friends in the church, but because of our own particular missionary lifestyle and frequent moves, those friends seldom became very close. We were in the United States, then in Manila, then back in the United States, then in Jerusalem, Israel, then in Hong Kong. By the time they got to know their friends fairly well, we were receiving a new outreach from God.

However, our sons made beautiful new friends in Hong Kong, in Jerusalem, and in Manila. But the greatest thing was that the boys became very close friends with each other. They were great at playing games among themselves. In Manila, we lived in a Spanish-style house beside the church. The yard was surrounded by a stone fence. Most of the time I found the boys playing by themselves in the yard.

I taught our sons to be gracious to the people wherever we lived and to enjoy their company. This they did and still retain delightful memories from around the world.

I also taught my sons to respect our total congregation, when I taught them that we must shepherd the whole flock. We could not afford to have intimate friendships with a select few members of the congregation. If we had become too close to some, we would have alienated others. That's why I have tried to be friends with the entire congregation, treating everyone alike.

My sons have adopted the same attitude toward friendships now that they are working in the ministry. They have friends within the congregation of our church in South Bend or among the staff of our organization. They also have fellowship with a wide range of Christians.

The second environment that is a factor in forming friendships is the neighborhood. For the ordinary boy or girl, the neighborhood becomes the primary environment for making friends and finding other children to play with. That is why it is so important when moving to a new city or neighborhood to select a place where your children will have desirable playmates nearby.

But again for the Sumrall boys, the neighborhood was not the primary place where they made friends. Those came from the church. Louise and I were careful not to allow our sons to associate too freely with children of unbelievers—at least not without specific guidance. We warned them of the spiritual condition of those families and pointed out that such homes were the breeding ground for drinking, smoking, bad language, and deep-seated attitudes that were contrary to the kingdom of God.

However, we were not legalistic about it. We did permit the boys to play in the neighborhood. Otherwise we might have had a rebellion on our hands. But by carefully explaining the reasons we did not want them to become too close to the neighborhood children—and by not permitting them to stay overnight in the homes of unbelievers—we were able to discourage them from forming close friendships with those who teach them evil deeds.

I do not believe our boys were overprotected, however. They still got to know the neighborhood children pretty well. They compared them with their friends at church, and they agreed with our counsel. They did not complain when we told them to come straight home from school. They were happy to be in a peaceful, nonargumentative home atmosphere where there was no lying and where there were people they could trust.

When they did play with the neighborhood children, they could be just as happy and natural as they were when playing with other children. Race or economic level was never a barrier. We taught our sons against discrimination on such bases. In the Philippines, the boys played with Filipino children; in Hong Kong there were Chinese and other Oriental children among their friends. During our six months in Israel, they played for hours with Israeli children who could not speak a word of English. Everywhere they got along well with the neighborhood children.

The only limits we put on our boys in terms of restricting their friendships were in keeping them from associating freely with families dominated by sin.

Because of their training, our boys developed a measure of independence in the neighborhood. We could trust them to be on their own without worrying about them.

When we lived in Hong Kong, for example, Stephen was taking music lessons. His teacher lived in Kowloon, across the harbor from the peak where we lived. Although Steve was only eleven, once a week he got on the bus by himself, rode down to the harbor, then took the ferry across the bay to Kowloon. He never had a bit of trouble.

We did not hide our boys or keep people away from them. The only thing we were trying to do was to inform them as much as possible about sin. We did this by telling them what sin is and what sinful people are like.

The third environment is the school. I feel it is extremely important to choose schools that will contribute favorably toward a child's eternal destiny—not draw him away from it and into sin.

In some of the early years of their education, our sons attended Christian schools, as in the Philippines and Jerusalem. We knew they were receiving good moral and spiritual guidance as well as getting an education. In the upper grades, however, we did what most Christian parents have to do: we sent our boys to public high schools.

Before school busing, the school environment depended on the neighborhood in which a family lives. Like other Christian families, we had to select the neighborhood where we were to live with consideration for the quality of the public schools. The school, the teachers, and the friends our children make in school can have a far-reaching influence on their moral and spiritual lives. What a tragedy when a child succumbs to peer and school pressure and questions the very foundations of his Christian beliefs.

I always recommend that Christian parents visit the schools their children attend and get to know the teachers and the principal. This includes carefully explaining to the teachers the importance one places on the children's spiritual welfare and development, and requesting that nothing be said or done in the classroom that would in any way belittle or degrade Christian spiritual values. That may seem a lot to ask, but it is one way of protecting our religious freedom. It is even a good idea to invite teachers home for refreshments so that they can begin to understand the home atmosphere from which the children come.

Teachers shape the thinking habits of their students. They greatly influence the way children formulate patterns of learning and living and the way they make decisions. Such things follow them throughout life. It is best to make sure—as much as humanly possible—that they are in the right school and have the right teachers.

As far as I know, the only place where our sons were laughed at because of being Christian was in the United States. Overseas, the fact that they were Christians seemed to be an added advantage. However, in Hong Kong they were teased in the British private school they attended because they were having difficulty reciting in class. Their teacher forced them to recite, using the British pronunciation and accent.

From my personal life experiences, I taught my sons that earthly friends can let you down. The only lasting friend we have—the One who will never let us down—is Jesus Christ. We need to develop our relationship with Him to such a degree that we can go to Him with all of our problems and cares, knowing that He is always ready to save us, to deliver us, and to lift us up.

After our heavenly friendship, we need to maintain the sanctity of our family. Family ties are the strongest relationships in the world, and we should do everything possible to keep them that way. This is why I believe so strongly in the need to save the American family. Without a strong family anchorage, the American society has begun to drift. A lot of loose relationships have been formed in which people do not know the meaning of the word *commitment*. People are living together without marrying, staying together as long as the relationship feels good or meets the person's own egocentric needs, and then breaking off to look for a new partner when things go sour. Those relationships do not survive difficult times.

I believe in having friends. I love being with people with whom I feel compatible—people whose company I can enjoy and with whom I can relax. We all need to have friends and to be friends. But we have to be careful that we do not "idolize" friends, treating them almost like gods.

Some may feel I am overemphasizing family ties to the detriment of other relationships, but I do not feel there is any conflict here. The family is still the basic unit of society, and everything should be done to preserve it.

My primary relationship is still with Jesus. All other relationships have to be secondary. Among my earthly relationships, the family has to come above others. I believe this attitude is actually a benefit and will help to strengthen our society, if others adopt it too.

These priorities, however, do not make people outside our family any less important to us. We value each and every person, and want to share as much of ourselves as possible in Christian fellowship.

I have not particularly formed intimate friendships within the congregations I have pastored, because I believe the pastor has to be a shepherd to the whole flock. However, I have developed close friendships with pastors and evangelists with whom I have worked. Those relationships developed while ministering and working together. The temporary nature of those joint ministries meant that separation was not far off, but our work together made memories for a lifetime. These we treasure.

9

Feeling Good—and Important

My family is a happy family.

Every Christian family can and should be happy. But it is not enough just to be a Christian family—there is a lot more that goes into producing happiness. I do not mean just having good times together, although that is part of it. I mean working together to maintain the proper attitudes that produce inner joy, peace, and a sense of well-being.

I am talking about things such as love and respect.

I am also referring to encouragement and praise.

We need to emphasize the positive side of family relationships. The family is meant to be the place where we can feel good about ourselves, where we are loved and uplifted and where we are encouraged to develop to our fullest potential.

It is a place where we can feel secure.

Before I even had a family, those were the things I was planning and praying for. And that is the kind of family God gave me.

It all began with the precious wife that God supplied— a wife who shared my interests and goals in the ministry, a wife who was just as concerned as I was that our children should be reared for God and give their lives to the ministry. She was literally an answer to prayer, a woman whose temperament and gifts complemented my own, making her a perfect companion and fellow laborer in the Lord. As I have said, our lives are so divinely blended that we have never had a serious argument or fight in forty years of marriage.

Our attitude toward the Christian home began with the way we treated each other. We were constantly thankful for what God had done in bringing us together, and we have continued to maintain that attitude of thankfulness.

Of course, Louise has not given me cause for complaint. Together we have prayed for and discussed having an exemplary Christian home. As a result of our role in the ministry, we often have many people come to our home. Because of that, we need to be presentable and above reproach. As a homemaker, Louise has been a gem. I cannot recall a time when our home was not orderly and clean, or when meals were not on the table at the prescribed time. Also, Louise has always been extremely careful about spending money. Louise has always been a full partner with me in ministry. She has been privy to all the information she needed to work alongside me and pray for the needs of whatever project or mission we were building at the time.

This is the kind of relationship into which we brought our three sons. As each of them came along, he began to share in all the concerns that Louise and I had. She and I often talked about the work of the Lord as we sat at the dinner table with the boys, and they got to see all the marvelous things God was doing. We always kept our conversation positive, stressing the things that God *was* doing, and praying for Him to deliver us from whatever problems were at hand. We never talked negatively at the table, nor did we discuss preachers or other people in a critical way.

A child measures his own feelings about himself primarily by the way his parents show they feel about him. If a father treats his son or daughter with contempt, the child will grow up with very little self-esteem. If a child feels his parents did not really want him in the first place, he will go through life feeling lonely and rejected.

Louise and I always tried to make sure our boys felt good about themselves. From their babyhood, we cuddled them and made them feel loved. Some of their earliest memories are of Mom and Dad telling them what a precious gift of God they were to us, and that they were equally as important to God. They knew they were wanted and needed, and that they were a blessing to us. I don't believe the thought has ever entered their heads that nobody cared about them. We always demonstrated that we did care.

I have seen so many fathers (and sometimes mothers) downgrade their children, not only to their faces but also in front of other people. I think it is a tragedy for parents to criticize a son or daughter when speaking to another person, or to criticize that child in front of another person. This not only lowers the child's self-esteem but also humiliates him and makes him feel like a nobody.

I have tried to earn the respect of my own sons by first respecting them. They are human beings created by God in His image. Although I am their human father who must rear and discipline them, I would be a hypocrite if I treated them as any less than the masterpieces of God's creations that they are.

Whenever I introduced my sons to people at church or at a meeting away from home, it was always on an equal basis with the others being introduced. They were never an afterthought, such as, "Oh, yes, and this is little Stephen, my son." The introduction was always up front: "Brother Jones, I'd like you to meet my son Stephen, who's a real help to his father in the ministry."

Whether my sons were eight years old or eighteen, they felt a part of my life and my work. They knew I was happy to introduce them, because they could feel the joy in my voice as I spoke.

Not only have I not downgraded my sons, but I have never permitted anyone else to downgrade them either— to their faces or otherwise. I let it be known that anything derogatory said about them or to them was a slap in my face too. My boys knew their daddy stood by them at all times.

The kind of respect I had for my sons allowed me to take them along to meetings where they could sit in on important discussions involving my ministry. They were introduced just as the rest of the people were, and they felt important. They knew they had the respect of others as well as the respect of their parents.

My sons have grown up with me in ministry. Today we still go to meetings together, but now it is often to important business discussions involving the various publishing and broadcasting activities of our ministry. It gives me great pleasure to sit back and see my sons holding their own in the midst of complex, sometimes delicate business negotiations. They are sure of themselves, and they know that I am behind them all the way. There have been many such meetings at which I have said hardly a word. My sons have developed a sense of self-assurance that does not require my being there to lean on.

Unfortunately, too many fathers today treat people outside the family with more concern than their own sons or daughters. They will go out of their way to aid a stranger or show some kind of Christian compassion, while their own children starve for affection and encouragement. This has never been the case in our home. Our boys come first, and they know we treat them as though they are the most important people in the world—which they are to us. In fact, I have always emphasized, "You are not just sons of Lester Sumrall. You are sons of God!"

Although my wife and I were strict in our discipline, we never tried to mold the boys into carbon copies of Lester Sumrall. That would have been impossible. After all, they have their own individual personalities. We encouraged them to express themselves freely to us and to one another, and not to hold their thoughts and feelings inside. The boys were never afraid of us, because they knew we loved them deeply.

Fear, of course, is from the devil, and a Christian should have no part of it. I frequently prayed over my sons and commanded fear to get away from them. As they got older, the boys took charge of their own prayer lives and stood against Satan whenever necessary. However, there were times when Dad still had to pray the prayer of faith over them.

Perhaps Frank was the most open in expressing himself and his feelings. The only time I recall his being particularly troubled was when we came back to the United States from overseas. He found that he was behind in some of his school subjects. He had to go to summer school to catch up, and that upset him.

One day when he was feeling particularly low, I simply told Frank, "You have to realize, son, that every man, from the president on down, puts his pants on the same way: one leg at a time. You're as good as anyone else, and you keep plugging away. You'll make it O.K."

He snapped out of it and refused to let it bother him after that.

In fact, nothing seems to bother Frank for very long. He is like a steaming teakettle, letting off steam as soon as the pressure begins to build up. If he ever thought we favored one of his brothers over him for any reason, he was quick to let us know.

Unlike Frank, Stephen does not express his feelings very openly. He is a lot like his mother in that regard. He remains cool, detached, observing what goes on around him while keeping his emotions under tight control.

Because of Steve's nature, I tried to encourage him to express himself and not take a back seat to anyone. That meant encouraging him through Bible college after he decided to go into the ministry, and praising him honestly for a good sermon when he preached.

From the time he was a child, Peter fixed broken things. He liked radios, then television. He worked the midnight shift on our twenty-four-hour radio station while attending college. He went to an engineering school and became a licensed television engineer. He was a natural for being the manager of all our radio and television stations.

Peter took over management responsibilities formerly carried out by men with long lists of credentials, both technical and managerial. At the time, he probably failed to realize that his eleven years of experience in television, plus his innate technical ability, more than qualified him for the position.

I am thankful that because we are a close family, Peter and I were able to discuss his problems, and I could give him the advice and encouragement he needed to operate large organizations.

Peter, as well as Frank and Stephen, is doing an excellent job for the total outreach ministry. They are being guided by the Holy Spirit and each is making a real contribution to this world ministry.

Today I see fire in the eyes of my three sons. They have caught the vision and are determined to help win those one million souls to Christ, as it was revealed to me by God.

From the time my sons were born I committed them to the Lord and gave them every opportunity to prepare for whatever part God had for them in the ministry. I knew they would need to be encouraged along the way, and I did as much as I could to help them both to feel good about themselves and to feel good about the ministry.

Because they are sons of God, I told them, they have been created for a purpose and have been endowed with gifts by the Holy Spirit to build His church. With God they can do anything! There are no impossibilities for God.

With their own eyes, my sons have seen how God has supplied the means to raise up new churches and other Christian ministries. They watched as God provided funds for a huge church in Manila, and they saw Him provide the finances for the whole church and television complex in South Bend when we started with no money at all. God has supplied everything we needed, and they know He will continue to supply what we need. My sons are very success-oriented when it comes to God's work.

Today I continue to encourage them to believe that they can do more than they ever anticipated. I am especially concerned that they keep on using the communications media—television, radio, and the printed word—as much as possible, because I believe it is through these means that many of those one million souls will be won to Christ.

They will do it.

They are sons of God, and He will provide.

10

Preparing for Leadership

One of the sad commentaries on leadership in the world today is the fact that almost all leaders fail to pass on their training and vision to their offspring. It is rare to see the leadership of great financial empires continue into the second or third generation. It is rarer still to see great government and political leaders succeeded in greatness by their sons. In the ministry, many of the sons of pastors seek other vocations.

I believe the reason is that fathers in such positions of authority do not take time to share their vision and their lives with their children. They are too busy leading political, financial, or religious institutions to devote time to guiding and teaching their own children. Therefore, the children never fully comprehend the talents and responsibilities required for leadership or catch the enthusiasm for pioneering and goal-reaching that is required for success.

From the time they were born, my sons were destined to become leaders. That was my goal for them.

You see, God had given me that vision of bringing to heaven one million immortal souls. This can only be achieved by bringing them to a faith in Jesus Christ. If the Lord tarries, my sons—successors—can bring another million souls to our Savior.

Success is not really success until it has produced and installed a successor. The full measure of success for Moses was in the training and installation of his successor, Joshua:

Now Joshua the son of Nun was full of the spirit of wisdom, for Moses had laid his hands upon him; so the children of Israel heeded him, and did as the LORD had commanded Moses. (Deut. 34:9)

Joshua had spent forty years as an assistant to Moses before that public ceremony at which Moses laid hands on his successor. It is true that Joshua was filled with the Holy Spirit, and that God worked miracles which showed the Israelites that Joshua indeed had the same power and authority as his predecessor. He had also learned from Moses much of what he needed to know about effective leadership.

Abraham was succeeded by Isaac, Isaac by Jacob; Moses by Joshua, David by Solomon; and Elijah by Elisha. In each of these cases the successor was prepared in advance to take over the responsibilities of leadership. They had qualified because of their intimate relationship with those they succeeded—in some cases a father, and in others a person who was a father figure to them.

Really effective leadership, I believe, is not just a technique to be learned, a set of principles to be followed, or a station in life that is automatically handed down from father to son. Instead, it requires instilling in the successor a powerful vision of what needs to be accomplished and why. Then it requires persuading the successor that he is the one chosen to accomplish the purpose for which he has been called.

In the ministry, this cannot always be predetermined by a human minister. I realize, as do most Christians, that one does not simply say, "I believe that one would make a good minister." Nor does the protegé aspire in human terms to become a minister. It is a calling, a choice by God.

But I also believe God would call many more if they were willing and prepared.

I wanted my boys to be willing and prepared. I believed that God would be pleased with me if I trained them to be ready for the ministry if He should choose to call them. From the time they were little boys, I told them how wonderful it was to serve the Lord Jesus. Our dinner conversation was always filled with the successes of the ministry and stories of those who had come to Christ or had been healed or delivered from evil spirits.

My sons experienced the thrill of the miraculous ways God was working in my ministry. In the Philippines, they could read in the daily newspapers the exciting story of deliverance, when I was called on to minister to a girl who was being literally bitten by demons. The story had been in the paper for days, telling how the police and medical personnel were dumbfounded and unable to help this pitiful girl. The doctors watched as her body produced terrible bite marks before their eyes, although no attacker was visible. When I was finally called in and succeeded in casting out the demons responsible for the attacks, my picture and stories about the incident were published in newspapers and magazines throughout the Philippines. At home, we rejoiced in God's mighty power and anointing. The boys understood the need for this ministry in the power of the Holy Spirit.

As I look back over the ways I provided my sons with an avenue toward leadership, it has become apparent to me that four factors were involved:

1. Example
2. Vision
3. Training
4. Opportunity

Each factor was singularly important, but it was necessary for all of them to interconnect to produce sons who would lead.

Primary among these factors is example.

Each of my sons today will tell you that he learned more about leadership by observing me than from any other education he had. By virtue of my ministry, I am a leader appointed by God to shepherd the flock He has given me. I am not a follower, nor have I ever been—except as a disciple of Jesus Christ.

While my sons were still quite young I told them, "Boys, there are two kinds of people in the world: leaders and followers. God has made me a leader, and I want you boys to be leaders, too."

They were in on everything I was doing—whether building up the ministry on the mission field or establishing the headquarters of the Lester Sumrall Evangelistic Association in South Bend. The trials and the triumphs were regular dinner table conversation topics, and the boys had their full share in speaking their minds. I never suppressed them. Although I am a compulsive talker, at the table I would listen and give them a chance to do the talking. I asked them for their opinions and let them give me their suggestions in a number of areas.

My sons knew the important details of the ministry wherever we were—the amount of money needed, the obstacles to be overcome in terms of time and manpower, and all of the other problems that crop up in establishing a new work. They knew I had the responsibility for getting the job done, because I was the one who had received the mandate from the Lord. Our sons felt that God's mandate to me was equally to them.

This type of relationship was not what I had personally experienced as a youth. My father had been completely the opposite in his approach to being a father. He was not a Christian at the time, so we did not pray together. Neither did we talk very much. Whatever aspirations, fears, or obstacles were on his mind, he kept pretty much to himself.

I simply did not want such a lack of communication to exist between me and my sons.

Many businessmen and pastors are the same way. They never tell their families—particularly their children—any of the day-to-day challenges and victories in their lives. Thus they deprive those closest to them of a significant portion of their lives.

This does not include giving the family all of the office gossip and revealing confidential information, because that would be a violation of trust in their leadership and it would have a negative effect on their children. However, I think pastors, especially, should tell their families how they see God working in the world and in the lives of those in the church. They need to share the ways He has helped them overcome significant obstacles along the way in building the ministry. This gives the family a sense of belonging and of contributing. That is what I provided for my sons. In effect, they became partners with me in ministry even from their youth.

The boys also learned something else from my example: No leader should be afraid to get his hands dirty.

A leader cannot force people to do the humbler tasks of ministry or of any other kind of vocation if the leader himself is unwilling to perform those duties. It is a well-known illustration in preaching that a shepherd does not follow his flock of sheep and bellow orders to them, nor does he stand off to one side and expect them to go where he directs them. Instead, he has to walk in front of them and show them the way.

In the work of the ministry I have had to put on my old clothes and do the work of a common laborer in order to help construct some of the church buildings for congregations I have pastored. I was working alongside my laymen, but I also was their leader. They were able to follow my example because I worked hardest of all. Sometimes I even had to be the church janitor. Whatever job needed to be done, I had to be willing to do it myself if necessary.

My sons have seen that. Today they are in positions of leadership, and they also are not above doing the more menial tasks for which they are responsible. My youngest son, Peter, said recently, "I can't force the people at the television station to work if I don't work. I work as hard as anyone. In fact, I work harder and put in longer hours."

You see, a leader cannot look upon himself as a "star" who gets all the credit while a lot of others labor thanklessly to keep him in his glory. I expect more of myself than of anyone else, and my sons have acquired the same attitude.

Too many people today want success without sacrifice and hard work, but it just does not come that way. Success has a price tag. That price tag is total commitment to the task at hand and to meeting the desired goal—whether in marriage, ministry, communications, or any other area of life or work than one can think of. Someone has to pay the price.

The second factor in developing leadership in my sons was giving them a vision.

106

I would not be where I am today in ministry if it had not been for the two visions God gave me when I was a teenager: the vision of the Bible and the casket that prompted me to give my heart to the Lord and become a preacher, and the vision of the unimaginable masses of humanity moving relentlessly toward eternal damnation and destruction because they had not received the gospel.

Not everyone receives visions like that. I have received only those two in my entire ministry. Anyone who aspires to leadership must become impelled by an overpowering conviction that something must be done, and that he is the person called to ensure that it is done.

The Bible says, "Where there is no revelation [vision] the people cast off restraint" (Prov. 29:18). The vision God gave me has sustained me to minister in over a hundred nations of the world. I have not grown weary or discouraged in the face of obstacles, because I know that God is able to complete any project He begins (see Phil. 1:6), using whatever instrument is available to Him. I have simply told Him I want to be that instrument.

My sons have not seen these same visions in the same way I have, yet over the years my visions have caught their own imaginations. This has produced an inner enthusiasm for commiting themselves to achieving the same goal that I have had all these years.

How did it happen? Did God have to speak to them in an audible voice to get their attention and spur them on? No, they have not needed the same manifestations, any more than every sinner needs the blinding-light appearance that Saul of Tarsus had in order to become a Christian. My sons have needed someone to proclaim the message of the visions to them, and I was the only person who could do that.

If they heard me talk about those visions once, they

heard it hundreds of times. They have heard me describe the terrible spiritual condition of our world today, but more than that, they see the conditions for themselves. Because we were missionaries, they had the opportunity to see firsthand the spiritual poverty of people in places such as the Orient, Europe, and the Middle East. They were in worship services when people were overcome with the conviction that they were sinners. With tears streaming down their faces, these people responded to the altar call by giving their hearts to Jesus Christ. They witnessed the authority of the name of Jesus in casting out demons.

To my sons, the ministry was never simply the preparation of sermons and the adminstration of a church. It was seeing a world in desperate need of salvation, and comprehending the amazing power that God had provided through the sacrifice of His Son and the gift of the Holy Spirit. They knew what Jesus meant when He told His disciples, "The harvest truly is plentiful, but the laborers are few. Therefore pray the Lord of the harvest to send out laborers into His harvest" (Matt. 9:37–38).

Today each of my sons has the same vision I have for reaching one million souls for Jesus. They have joined me in the ministry, not to help me build an organizational empire but to do everything possible to ensure that we are following God's direction in proclaiming the gospel.

The third factor in leadership is training.

Perhaps there is such a thing as a born leader, but most of the time, leadership is a learned ability. As early as my sons were able, I allowed them to take part in my ministry and to get the feel of being in front of people. They sang on my radio program and on television, and they sang in the church. They spoke with me from the pulpit. They got to see leadership from my perspective, not from that of the congregation. When they were old enough, they led youth groups and other activities in the church.

At home, we all read books about well-known leaders—especially those whose leadership was passed down to their descendants. We read about the Rothschilds. The boys were as fascinated as I was with the story of how one old father, living in a Polish ghetto, could instill in his sons the vision for gaining enormous international influence by getting into leadership in banking. The sons obeyed him and moved into banking in England, France, and Germany, where they eventually acquired the enormous success and influence their father had predicted.

We read about the Rockefellers and the Kennedys, and a whole host of other famous families. We discussed what we could learn both from their failures and their successes. We read about the Chinese and learned how they loved and cared for one another within families. We saw how family relationships provided great strength for individuals.

We discussed what we had read. We analyzed, critiqued, and evaluated. Not all of the things we learned were applicable to Christian life and ministry, but those that were, we examined to see how we could use them. From those biographies my sons learned many of the principles of leadership that allowed them to move naturally into positions within our ministry.

I also taught them to be observers, just as I am an observer. One can learn a lot about leadership by watching how others lead. When I was a young man, I learned much from observing Howard Carter, the British scholar and teacher I ministered with around the world. In turn, my sons learned a lot about leadership by observing what I did.

Together we discussed management principles—how to

treat people within an organization, how to judge loyalty and to discern what a person is loyal to. There is a lot of common sense involved in management, and that is not something that can be learned readily. It is intuitive, and I believed my sons had common sense. I encouraged them to develop it.

I also taught them to be decision makers, and to base their decisions on facts—not hearsay. I told them to be careful not to rush into a decision. A fool will run off half-cocked and make a poor decision. A wise man will wait until he has all the data before he makes his decision.

Finally, to become a leader, one must have the opportunity.

Of course, if a person is a born leader or has a compelling vision for reaching some goal, he will make his own opportunities. The kind of leadership I wanted for my sons was in the ministry I had already developed. I wanted to make that available to them if they wanted it.

While they were still going to school, the boys were already being given opportunities to work in various places within the ministry. Whether it was in our church, our Bible school, or one of our communications facilities, they started at the bottom, doing such chores as sweeping, mopping, and cleaning up.

Little by little they worked their way up as they gained experience and ability. When they were still teenagers I discouraged their going to secular places of employment in order to earn extra money. There was always plenty to be done at the church complex, and I felt my boys could do the jobs as well as anyone else.

After completing their formal education, they were still given the opportunity of continuing to work in the ministry. They had seen my example, had caught the vision for reaching one million souls for Jesus Christ, and had qualified for leadership through training. It was natural for them to choose to take advantage of the opportunity I held out to them. Pushing them was not necessary.

I was giving them not only an opportunity but also a heritage. They did not have to start where I had in the ministry and build it up from nothing. They could start where I was and continue building on the foundation that had already been laid.

Both Frank and Stephen went to Bible college to prepare for the ministry. Both of them wanted to be missionaries after graduation, and it was only fitting that they should take advantage of the opportunities to be missionaries from our own church. Frank ministered in Indonesia, while Stephen went to Alaska and South America to preach.

Peter chose to labor for Christ by directing all our ministry in electronics and television. This was the vehicle he used to help us reach our modern world for Christ.

Today there are many ministries as well as many businesses controlled by men with vision. Yet I wonder what will become of their organizations when they retire or die. I believe a large percentage of them will pass into other hands and will be controlled by people with a much different vision.

I know of one organization involved in Christian communications where the children of the president are not involved in any managerial capacity. They have not been brought up that way. In fact, their father will not allow his family to have any decision-making role in the organization. So his son watches him from a fairly low-level vantage point in the business. The young man is known for his sarcastic attitude toward his father.

I also know of a major department store chain that was built up by one man with vision. Today that chain is being sold because none of the sons is interested in the business. They have taken advantage of their father's money and prestige to devote themselves to lives of thrill-seeking elsewhere.

I did not want that to happen to me or my organization. I made sure my sons received the kind of guidance and direction that would enable them to succeed me in ministry, if they were called by God to do so. Now that preparation is paying off. As each of my sons has matured and gained experience, he has moved up into leadership within the organization. Our ministry is large enough to provide places for all three of them.

Today I look back on that guidance with satisfaction. Frank, Stephen, and Peter are already running most of the organizations as if I were not here. They make mistakes, of course, but that is to be expected. I have to look at the kind of decisions I was making when I was the same age, and I must admit I made some stupid ones! When I look back on my own ministry and compare their decision-making ability with mine at about the same age, I see that so far, they are way ahead of me! Oh, yes, I sometimes have to caution them, based on my greater experience, but they now have assumed most of the decision-making responsibilities, thus leaving me free to concentrate on ministering to the world.

I am confident the future of LESEA, Incorporated, is in good hands.

11

Helping Them to Choose

One of the most important things a parent needs to realize is that each child is an individual. As much as we want to guide our children and shape their lives, we cannot violate their individuality. If we tried too hard to plan their lives for them, we might stifle some special abilities or talents given to them by God. Or we might simply have a rebellion on our hands.

One reason I have been successful in bringing up my sons is that I allowed them to be themselves. Yes, I disciplined them and guided them carefully, but I never tried to mold them into three little Lester Sumralls who would be merely carbon copies of their daddy.

All along I hoped they would take over my ministry. I prayed for that. I encouraged them in that direction, but I never blatantly pressured them. If they had wanted to do something else, I could not have stopped them, although I would have been very disappointed.

As it turned out, all three of my sons chose to work in my ministry. I did not have to coax or plead. It is what they wanted to do.

However, their choices were not made in a vacuum. My influence was there, whether they realized it or not. I always encouraged them to see the possibilities of the ministry God had given me. I made it clear they could probably go farther in my evangelistic organization than anywhere else.

I let them understand that they could follow me into the ministry without having to mirror the image of their father. They could do it their own way.

Therefore, my sons had to see in me the ingredients of an ordinary man—someone they could emulate without fear that they could not attain my position in the ministry. Many children of "public figures" shrink back from following in their parents' footsteps because they are afraid they can never match the image and reputation that has already been established.

A minister cannot afford to assume a "star" attitude. One of the greatest deceptions of Satan is to make a pastor think the flock is following him rather than Jesus. Pretty soon he can have the flock going off in the wrong direction.

The three hooks the devil uses to catch preachers and cause them to fall are self-exaltation, greed for material gain, and sex. Thinking of himself as a star is the first step on the way to a pastor's downfall.

I have never wanted to be a star, nor have I wanted anyone else to think of me in that light—least of all my sons. To them I have always been just a daddy, the father who loves them and provides for them by putting bread on the table and buying them things they like.

A father cannot be a star in his own household. The family sees him as he really is: a man who needs to shave and brush his teeth in the morning, who expresses feelings of joy or sorrow that the congregation knows nothing about, who is weak in the face of a crisis and needs to draw on the strength and courage of Jesus.

A man's family sees him when he is down, as well as

when he is up. They know he is just another human being like themselves. He needs to do the chores at home, play with the children, encourage and love his wife, and pay the bills. These are down-to-earth responsibilities—not star performances.

I wanted my sons to see the public ministry not as performance on a stage but as a necessary means of fulfilling the vision God had given me. They were involved in the ministry from the time they were in kindergarten, and they came to see it from my perspective. It was never anything awesome to them.

They also knew I was constantly in a battle against Satan, and my sons always prayed for me. In fact, I asked them to pray for me. They saw that I was not performing out there as a result of my own strength when I preached and ministered to the people. It was the Lord Jesus Christ working through me, and I was just being obedient to Him.

Even with their involvement in the ministry from a very early age, there was no guarantee that Frank, Stephen, or Peter would choose to come into the ministry when he grew up. That is why I had to give each of them encouragement along the way. I had to show them the need for the ministry and then persuade them that the work of the Lord was as important a vocation as they could ever choose.

In spite of all of this, however, I could not push them. A father cannot dictate to his children the professions they are to pursue. A lot of parents have made that mistake, only to have the children rebel and go in some other direction.

One of the most important ways I guided my sons into the ministry was in helping them to choose the right college.

For a long time I had admired Elim Bible Institute in Lima, New York, because I felt it was a solid charismatic school that produced enthusiastic missionaries and preachers without limiting them to any one denominational doctrine or point of view. However, I did not force my sons to go there.

I did not tell Frank, "Son, you are going to attend Elim Bible Institute." Instead, I made sure he was supplied with all the information I could get about the school. As we were nearing the time when a decision had to be made, I drove Frank to Lima for a tour of the Elim campus. We looked over all of the facilities.

After all of that, he could still have decided to go elsewhere, but Frank liked what he saw. In the end he chose Elim himself.

From the time he was five years old, Frank had known he wanted to become a minister. I believe he admired his daddy's preaching. But his call definitely was from the Lord. The only time the choice of vocation came into question was briefly while he was in high school. He loved history, and at one point he said he might like to become a history teacher. However, the call to the ministry was just too strong, and the thoughts of teaching history gradually faded away. I must say I was gratified when he made the decision to go into the ministry—and to prepare for it at Elim.

In each of my sons, I was looking for the marks of successors. Frank seemed a natural—not only because he looked and sounded more like me than his brothers did, but also because his calling to the ministry had come early in life. Throughout life, he wanted to be like me. I would have been very surprised if he had chosen a career other than the ministry.

With Stephen, however, it was not as clear. His quiet

nature was not a problem, because that certainly is no barrier to the ministry. But initially his interests leaned toward the area of business. He was interested in things such as mathematics and accounting, and he favored those courses in high school.

Later, like Frank, Stephen caught the vision for the ministry. When it came time to go to college, there was no doubt about his choice. He wanted to follow his brother to Elim. There was no need for pressure or persuasion.

When it came to the youngest, Peter, it was a more gradual process. His interests were in mechanical and electronic things. When he was only fourteen, he removed the motor from an oil-burning 1963 Rambler that someone had left with him. During the winter he took the whole thing apart and scattered pieces of the engine all through the basement. Louise had a terrible time getting down there to do the laundry, but he was enjoying himself so we let him go ahead. By the following spring he had totally overhauled and reassembled the engine. He even spent a couple of hundred dollars of his own money to fix it. Then he turned around and sold the car for only twenty-five dollars. He said he just wanted the experience.

As his high school graduation neared, I began talking to Peter about his future. He was already working at our radio station in South Bend. He was doing a hard job as a disc jockey on the four-to-midnight shift, and he loved everything about radio.

Peter chose Bethel College, a church-related school in the South Bend area, and took their broadcasting courses.

I discussed with Peter the advantages of being able to continue living at home and working at the television station, which he loved. Even so, after completing his freshman year at Bethel with ease, he found that he could get all the credentials he needed to pursue a career in radio and television without having to spend three more years in college. What he wanted was a engineer's license, for which he would have to take a federal examination. He could prepare for that in a special television school in Florida.

Now each of my sons was in a position to decide what he wanted to do with the rest of his life. Of course, I hoped all of them would choose to join me in LESEA, but there was no guarantee. I had been priming them all their lives for the day they would make that decision, but each of them had to make the choice by his own free will.

I rejoice that all three chose to join me. No persuasion was needed.

At last I had the satisfaction of seeing all my preparation come to fruition. I felt I had been faithful to God in training my sons, and God Himself had worked in each of them to bring them into the ministry.

Frank joined the staff of the Christian Center as associate pastor. There his natural talents began to unfold. He is an excellent inspirational preacher.

Frank not only has followed me into the preaching ministry, but also has assumed many of the pastoral duties at the church. I do not have to supervise him, because he is his own man. When he teaches in our World Harvest Bible College, he teaches the subjects his way—the biblical way.

Besides being associate pastor of the church, Frank also assists me on our daily television program, "Today with Lester Sumrall." He often prays for the needs of viewers that have been mailed or phoned in to the station. He also teaches regularly on radio.

Although Steve is ordained to the ministry, God has led

him into our organization in a somewhat different capacity. Steve saw the need for someone to take over the administrative duties of the ministry, and that is what he offered to do. It was an obvious choice, because he had been interested in all the aspects of running a business from the time he was in high school.

Steve became office manager for LESEA, and he also began to carry his own share of pastoral duties at the church. He shares preaching duties with Frank when I am out of town. From the beginning, Steve has been the co-host on my daily television program. He also produces his own television program which is viewed nationwide.

Steve is more a teacher than an evangelist. He has a calm, even delivery and a quiet manner that bespeaks expertise. He has already made a number of teaching videotapes for television. He also shares in our teaching seminars at the church and teaches at the World Harvest Bible School. Sometimes he and Frank teach seminars in various cities around the country.

Perhaps Steve's strongest love lies in the area of business management. When he felt I was overburdened with work, he was able to step in and keep everything operating smoothly.

As the ministry grew, it became obvious that Steve was the logical person to be in charge of the administrative duties. He is now president of LESEA, Inc.

With Peter's interest and abilities in radio and television, there was no question about the role he was to play in the ministry. Although he took time out in the fall of 1973 to travel to Southeast Asia with the singing group "The Living Sound" as their sound engineer, he quickly returned to the television stations and has been working there steadily in various capacities since then.

At one point, while working as a station engineer,

Peter had a real desire to see better Christian programs produced. With my permission, he changed positions and found that he thoroughly enjoyed being production manager of the program.

Peter is a hard worker. He concentrated on improving the quality of our television production. He earned his promotions through hard work and demonstrated ability. When given the option of hiring someone from outside or allowing Peter to move up in the organization, the choice to me was obvious.

Peter has continued to move up in the station management. Today he is general manager of our television stations in South Bend and Indianapolis and of WHME radio. He had worked at the stations for eleven years before taking over top management, and he knows the radio and television business inside and out. Our stations run smoothly and professionally, and Peter has an enthusiastic and well-coordinated staff.

I deeply realize that I have not put together the LESEA ministry and staff that runs it through my own efforts—this is God's ministry. I certainly did not "give" my sons their positions of leadership. All of this has been accomplished spiritually under the guidance of the Holy Spirit.

I could not have planned it to work out this way if I had tried. It is impossible to control individual lives that way. Each of my sons has a mind of his own and has made his own decisions.

Yes, I encouraged them and guided them. Yes, I provided opportunities for them. Still, it was God who worked it all out. He put together the pieces of this miraculous jigsaw puzzle in a way that outshines anything I could have foreseen.

Frank is a pastor with definite gifts of the Spirit for leading our local congregation. He also conducts crusades in various cities around the country.

Stephen has blossomed as the administrator of the business, educational, and publishing activities of LESEA. In addition, he has his own television program and preaches in various cities in the evangelistic ministry.

Peter is in charge of all electronic communications. He has a vital role in our world ministry, sending videotapes of our program to Japan and elsewhere, and overseeing our hookups with the satellite networks.

To me this is a miracle. Only God could have known I would have a world-wide ministry and an organization that would require three top managers who totally love the visions of God. Only God could have given me three sons who would fit those spots without my demanding it. It is not a Sumrall empire, but rather a highly efficient, evangelistic organization designed to reach a million souls for Christ.

I praise God. Only He could have designed it.

12

Some Good Advice

Recently a visitor to our church engaged in a conversation with Frank's ten-year-old son, Lester. Lester is a very outgoing, inquisitive child. He wanted to know all about the visitor's background, his occupation, and so on.

Finally the visitor asked, "Well, Lester, what are you going to do when you grow up?"

"Take over."

The visitor was surprised by such bold self-assurance.

"Do you mean take over this ministry?" he asked the boy.

"Yep."

"That's an awfully big responsibility, isn't it?"

"Yep."

"Do you think you'll be ready for it?"

"Yep."

With that, Lester jumped onto his bicycle and pedaled off across the parking lot, leaving the visitor shaking his head.

Until then, I had not known my grandson was so certain of his potential future role in the ministry, but I am not surprised. That is the kind of attitude I had tried to instill in my sons. Now my grandchildren are catching the same vision.

I am assured that this ministry will continue in the second generation, and I pray in the third as well, if Jesus tarries. We will experience success in our efforts to reach those million souls for Christ, if we continue to carry the same vision and consecration.

Men who do not make provision for successors in business or ministry often leave behind problems that someone else has to clear up. Either that, or they leave no business or ministry at all. I feel that God will give a smooth transition for my successors, as I have provided them with an organization that can expand and grow. Instead of a mess, I will leave behind a well-organized, expertly managed evangelistic ministry.

My sons will not have to struggle to match my accomplishments in the ministry either. They have developed a working relationship together that will far exceed anything I could accomplish alone.

While I am still on earth, I will continue to lead this ministry and work with all my strength to fulfill my commission from God. As long as I am able, I will also continue to counsel my sons in their roles in the ministry and encourage them on to greater accomplishments as God leads.

There will come a time, however, when I will no longer be here to give advice. I can imagine my sons facing some dilemma in the ministry and asking one another, "What would Dad have done in this situation?"

I wish I could leave behind all the answers, but I cannot. In fact, that will not be necessary. I know the Holy Spirit is already guiding my sons as He has guided me. They will always have Him to turn to whenever they are not sure of the way.

I do have a few guidelines that I am leaving with them,

and they are guidelines that I would recommend to other Christians as well.

Here they are:

1. Be careful in forming human friendships. Although we need to make friends, it is rare in the world today to find friends who will become as faithful or more faithful than members of one's own family. From my own experience, I know that even the closest of friendships can end for a number of reasons: disagreements, embarrassment over some behavior, changes in religious or doctrinal beliefs, or simply separation when one or the other moves a good distance away to another city or state. If we plan our lives around human friends, we are in danger of being deeply disappointed.

2. If you go into any business, try to do it with your brothers or other close members of the family. That will strengthen the family. Because we are a family committed to winning souls for Jesus Christ, we need to keep our family strong by loving one another and helping one another through all of the obstacles of life.

3. Owe no one anything. If you cannot afford to pay cash for what you want, delay the purchase until you have the money. We live in an era of easy credit, but many a business or ministry has foundered because of debts they could not handle. The devil will use any means at his disposal to obstruct the work of the church, and debts can only be a drag on the ministry. Rather than pay interest, it would be much better to put that money into something that would profit the church.

4. Grow spiritually. That means reading the Bible and praying daily, and attending worship regularly. If we ever stop growing spiritually, we will begin to backslide. Sooner or later we will become an open target for Satan, who will tempt us in areas that will lead us away from the ministry or away from an effective witness of Jesus

Christ. The best protection against that is prayer, the Word, and strong Christian fellowship.

5. Be kind to all men. The Bible tells us that we are to love even our enemies and to do good to those who would persecute us. How much more important it is to make all the friends we can and to be well-regarded by all. A person will be a friend to you if you have already been a friend to him. Never pass up an opportunity to be a friend.

6. Respect seniority. Regardless of whether it is in business, politics, or the church, those who are older have learned much through their long experience. They are worth consulting and acknowledging for their wisdom. If you show respect for your elders, you will later reap what you sow. Someday you will enjoy the respect of those younger than yourself.

7. Highly respect all members of your family. It is too easy to speak disdainfully to those you see a lot. It is easy to blame them for negative situations. If allowed to continue, such internal bickering can lead to a weakening and disintegration of the family. Instead, be quick to forgive, quick to laugh with them, and quick to forget an insult or injury. Most of all, be quick to pray for one another.

8. Stay on the path. That path can sometimes be a very lonely road. When we want to live for Jesus, we will meet various trials. The road has its bends, hills, valleys, and stretches of roughness. At times we call out for human assistance, but there is none in sight and none that's effective. However, we can look to Jesus and find "a friend who sticks closer than a brother" (Prov. 18:24).

Look to Jesus.

Don't waver.

Don't quit.

God will see you through!